HIKING SLOVENIA'S JULIANA TRAIL

THREE-WEEK TREK: TRIGLAV NATIONAL PARK, BLED AND THE JULIAN ALPS

By Rudolf Abraham

JUNIPER HOUSE, MURLEY MOSS,
OXENHOLME ROAD, KENDAL, CUMBRIA LA9 7RL
www.cicerone.co.uk

MIX
Paper | Supporting
responsible forestry
FSC® C010256

Printed in China on responsibly sourced paper on behalf of Latitude Press Ltd
A catalogue record for this book is available from the British Library.
All photographs are by the author unless otherwise stated.

Route mapping by Lovell Johns www.lovelljohns.com
Contains OpenStreetMap.org data © OpenStreetMap
contributors, CC-BY-SA. NASA relief data courtesy of ESRI

For my daughter Tamara

Updates to this guide

While every effort is made by our authors to ensure the accuracy of guide-books as they go to print, changes can occur during the lifetime of an edition. Any updates that we know of for this guide will be on the Cicerone website (www.cicerone.co.uk/1088/updates), so please check before planning your trip. We also advise that you check information about such things as transport, accommodation and shops locally. Even rights of way can be altered over time.

The route maps in this guide are derived from publicly available data, databases and crowd-sourced data. As such they have not been through the detailed checking procedures that would generally be applied to a published map from an official mapping agency, although naturally we have reviewed them closely in the light of local knowledge as part of the preparation of this guide.

We are always grateful for information about any discrepancies between a guidebook and the facts on the ground, sent by email to updates@cicerone.co.uk or by post to Cicerone, Juniper House, Murley Moss, Oxenholme Road, Kendal, LA9 7RL.

Register your book: To sign up to receive free updates, special offers and GPX files where available, register your book at www.cicerone.co.uk.

Front cover: 15th-century church on an island on Lake Bled

CONTENTS

Map key 6
Mountain safety 7
Route summary table 8–9

INTRODUCTION 11
Key facts and figures. 12
The Juliana Trail 13
Geography and geology 15
Climate. 15
When to hike 17
Wildlife and plants 18
Triglav National Park 21
History 22
Getting to Slovenia. 27
Public transport in the Julian Alps. 28
Accommodation. 29
Food and drink. 30
Language 32
Money 32
Phones 32
Public holidays. 32
Hiking the Juliana Trail 33
Maps and apps. 35
Water 35
Hiking with kids 36
Low impact hiking 36
Safety and emergencies 36
Using this guide 38

THE JULIANA TRAIL 39
Stage 1   Kranjska Gora to Mojstrana. 40
Side trip   Peričnik Waterfalls 47
Stage 2   Mojstrana to Jesenice 49
Stage 3   Jesenice to Begunje. 55
Stage 4   Begunje to Bled. 63
Side trip   Vintgar Gorge 70

Dawn view of the Martuljek group from Srednji vrh after November snowfall (Stage 1)

Stage 5   Bled to Goreljek na Pokljuki 73
Stage 6   Goreljak na Pokljuki to Stara Fužina 79
Side trip   Lake Bohinj and Savica Waterfall 84
Stage 7   Stara Fužina to Bohinjska Bistrica 86
Stage 8   Bohinjska Bistrica to Podbrdo 92
Stage 9   Podbrdo to Grahovo ob Bači 97
Stage 10   Grahovo ob Bači to Most na Soči 102
Stage 11   Most na Soči to Tolmin 106
Side trip   Tolmin Gorges. 110
Stage 12   Tolmin to Kobarid 113
Side trip   Kozjak Waterfall and the Kobarid Historical Trail. 119
Stage 13   Kobarid to Bovec. 121
Side trip   Soča Gorge. 127
Stage 14   Bovec to Log pod Mangartom 129
Stage 15   Log pod Mangartom to Tarvisio 134
Stage 16   Tarvisio to Kranjska Gora 142

BRDA EXTENSION. 149
Stage 17   Tolmin to Planinski dom pod Ježo 150
Stage 18   Planinski dom pod Ježo to Korada. 155
Stage 19   Korada to Šmartno. 161
Stage 20   Šmartno to Solkan. 165

Appendix A   Gateway city – Ljubljana 173
Appendix B   Language notes and glossary 174
Appendix C   Further reading. 184
Appendix D   Contacts and addresses. 185

Acknowledgements

This book could not have been written without the generous support, knowledge and enthusiasm of a number of people in Slovenia. My sincere thanks to Klemen Langus, Director at Tourism Bohinj and one of the main figures behind the Juliana Trail; Martin Šolar, Director of the Kobarid Museum, former Director of Triglav National Park and a fount of knowledge on the Julian Alps; Aleksandra Lipej, Global Communications Manager at the Slovenian Tourist Board; Viljam Kvalič, Director at Soča Valley Tourism; and Janko Humar, former Director at Soča Valley Tourism. Thanks also to Tine Murn, Blaž Veber, Tomaž Rogelj, Sašo Gašperin, Grega Šilc, Tomaž Bregant, Maša Klavora, Katja Drobnič, Leon Četrtič and Aleksandra Jezeršek Matjašič. Hvala vsem.

Symbols used on route maps

~~	route
- -~ -	alternative route
(S)	start point
(F)	finish point
(SF)	start/finish point
➤	route direction
~~	4 x 4 vehicle track
	woodland
	urban areas
	international border
....	motorway in tunnel
━■━	station/railway
	railway line in tunnel
=	bridge
▲	peak
⌂	accommodation
🏠	mountain hut/refuge serving food
🛆	campsite
■	building
⸸	church/chapel
⸸	monastery
⋒	castle
ⓘ	tourist information
⸈	waterfall
•	water feature
🚡 🚠	cable car/cable car station
P	car park
🍴	restaurant/café
†	wayside shrine
⊜	traditional boat
•	other feature

Relief
in metres

3200 and above	
3000–3200	
2800–3000	
2600–2800	
2400–2600	
2200–2400	
2000–2200	
1800–2000	
1600–1800	
1400–1600	
1200–1400	
1000–1200	
800–1000	
600–800	
400–600	
200–400	
0–200	

✳	viewpoint
⤳	pass
M	museum
■	bus stop
⊕	grocery

SCALE: 1:50,000

0 kilometres 0.5   1

0 miles   0.5

Contour lines are
drawn at 25m intervals
and highlighted at
100m intervals.

GPX files for all routes can be downloaded free at www.cicerone.co.uk/1088/GPX.

Mountain safety

Every mountain walk has its dangers, and those described in this guidebook are no exception. All who walk or climb in the mountains should recognise this and take responsibility for themselves and their companions along the way. The author and publisher have made every effort to ensure that the information contained in this guide was correct when it went to press, but, except for any liability that cannot be excluded by law, they cannot accept responsibility for any loss, injury or inconvenience sustained by any person using this book.

International distress signal *(emergency only)*
Six blasts on a whistle (and flashes with a torch after dark) spaced evenly for one minute, followed by a minute's pause. Repeat until an answer is received. The response is three signals per minute followed by a minute's pause.

Helicopter rescue
The following signals are used to communicate with a helicopter:

 Help needed:
raise both arms
above head to
form a 'Y'

 Help not needed:
raise one arm
above head, extend
other arm downward

Emergency telephone number
GRZS (Društvo Gorska reševalna služba): tel 112

Mountain rescue can be very expensive – be adequately insured.

ROUTE SUMMARY TABLE

Stage	Start/finish	Distance	Ascent/descent	Time	Page
1	Kranjska Gora to Mojstrana	18.5km	+325m/-595m	6hrs	40
Side trip	Mojstrana	12km	+250m/-250m	2hrs 30mins	47
2	Mojstrana to Jesenice	21km	+690m/-785m	6hrs 15mins	49
3	Jesenice to Begunje	17.5km	+465m/-460m	5hrs	55
4	Begunje to Bled	15km	+95m/-180m	4hrs	63
Side trip	Podhom to Zasip	5.5km	+175m/-175m	1hr 50mins	70
5	Bled to Goreljak na Pokljuki	21.5km	+870m/-105m	6hrs 30mins	73
6	Goreljak na Pokljuki to Stara Fužina	22km	+330m/-1050m	7hrs	79
Side trip	Stara Fužina	20km	+320m/-320m	4hrs 30mins	84
7	Stara Fužina to Bohinjska Bistrica	11km	+105m/-155m	3hrs	86
8	Bohinjska Bistrica to Podbrdo	14.5km	+770m/-785m	6hrs	92
9	Podbrdo to Grahovo ob Bači	18km	+1110m/-1210m	6hrs	97
10	Grahovo ob Bači to Most na Soči	19.5km	+870m/-1020m	6hrs 30mins	102
11	Most na Soči to Tolmin	8km	+205m/-160m	2hrs 30mins	106
Side trip	Tolmin	7.5km	+215m/-215m	2hrs	110
12	Tolmin to Kobarid	17km	+125m/-80m	4hrs	113
Side trip	Kobarid	9km	+285m/-285m	3hrs	119

Stage	Start/finish	Distance	Ascent/descent	Time	Page
13	Kobarid to Bovec	21km	+445m/-230m	7hrs	121
Side trip	Bovec	21km	+240m/-240m	6hrs	127
14	Bovec to Log pod Mangartom	12km	+340m/-150m	4hrs	129
15	Log pod Mangartom to Tarvisio	22km	+665m/-560m	7hrs	134
16	Tarvisio to Kranjska Gora	19.5km	+180m/-130m	5hrs	142
17	Tolmin to Planinski dom pod Ježo	13km	+1000m/-450m	5hrs	150
18	Planinski dom pod Ježo to Korada	20.5km	+720m/-670m	7hrs	155
19	Korada to Šmartno	11.5km	+60m/-620m	2hrs 45mins	161
20	Šmartno to Solkan	15km	+460m/-610m	4hrs 30mins	165

River Soča from the Napoleon Bridge below Kobarid (Stage 12)

INTRODUCTION

View across the Goriška Brda wine region from Šmartno (Stage 19)

The Juliana Trail is an outstanding long-distance hiking trail through Slovenia's Julian Alps, which makes a circuit of the country's highest mountain, Triglav. Designed to reduce the strain of visitor numbers on Triglav – which lies at the centre of Slovenia's most popular hiking area, and suffers increasingly from overcrowding and trail erosion – the Juliana makes a 270km circuit around this iconic 2864m peak, without actually climbing it, while a further 60km extension to the trail branches off to the south.

Rather than the usual two-day blitz on Triglav, the Juliana encourages visitors to stay longer and explore the surrounding area – which after all is equally beautiful, even if it is a few metres lower than the maximum altitude which rather arbitrarily defines a country's highest point.

Spread over 20 stages, its route takes in several less well-known valleys (meaning you'll meet fewer hikers along the trail), makes a few unexpected turns and even ducks over the border into Italy for a stage, while still managing to include such must-see spots as Bled, with its lakeside castle perched on a crag and picture-perfect island church. It crams in a whole slew of historical interest – from medieval castles, to a long history of iron working, and haunting relics from World War 1 (WW1) – and takes in some of the most exquisitely beautiful stretches of landscape you are likely to find anywhere. The trail is relatively easy – far more so than the Slovenian Mountain Trail, for example – with no technical sections, and stages end in villages and small towns where there is generally a good range of accommodation. The opportunities for seeing wildlife and wildflowers along the trail are amazing. And even though it doesn't climb Triglav, the Juliana still offers several fabulous views of the country's most famous mountain – which according to popular tradition, every true Slovene should climb at least once.

The Juliana hopes to reduce overcrowding on Triglav while still offering a very rewarding and memorable hiking experience, but the central idea behind the trail is the principle of sustainable development, and the preservation of rural settlements. The Julian Alps have an ageing population base, and an increasing number of people are turning away from working the land. And in the end, as Klemen Langus, one of the main figures behind developing the Juliana told me with a shrug over a beer in Bohinjska Bistrica, after a day's hiking across the trails around Lake Bohinj – if everybody ends up working in towns, if living in these mountain villages is no longer sustainable, then who will look after the land?

Encouraging sustainable tourism over a wider area rather than just in the immediate surroundings of Triglav,

and taking some of the route outside the national park, has the obvious benefit of spreading the money generated through tourism to local communities across a wider area. And as much as possible, the route was chosen to be accessible by public transport – great for getting to the route, or splitting it over two trips, but also a way to help keep that local infrastructure alive, since more hikers using buses means those services are more likely to continue running and benefit locals.

I first hiked some of the trails which would later become the Juliana back in the late 1990s, when I was living just over the border in neighbouring Croatia – and have been returning to hike in this breathtakingly beautiful corner of Europe ever since. Over the years I have never tired of exploring these mountains at the crossroads of central Europe and the Adriatic – whether walking beside the emerald green of the River Soča, or marvelling at its gorges and waterfalls, watching salamanders emerge to crawl across mossy paths after rain and clouds of butterflies amid Alpine pastures, or the bluish light of dawn on the Martuljek group from Srednji vrh. The Julian Alps never disappoint.

KEY FACTS AND FIGURES

- Country name: Republic of Slovenia (Republika Slovenija)
- Capital: Ljubljana
- Population: 2.1 million

- Land surface area: 20,273km^2
- National parks: Triglav National Park
- Language: Slovene
- Currency: Euro
- Time zone: GMT +1 (CET)
- International dialling code: +386
- Electricity: 220V/50Hz (standard European two-pin plug)

THE JULIANA TRAIL

From Kranjska Gora, the Juliana follows the left bank of the Sava Dolinka, climbing to Srednji vrh, from where there are jaw-dropping views south of the jumble of spiky peaks which make up the Martuljek group. From here it drops down to the village of Gozd Martuljek, and from there heads downstream to Mojstrana, at the entrance to the Vrata Valley. It climbs above Zagošni vrh for more superlative views, before perhaps rather unexpectedly heading into the industrial town of Jesenice, with its long history of mining and ironworking – a place way off the radar of most visitors to Slovenia, perhaps even more particularly those on a hiking trip.

Further southeast, the trail passes through Breznica, where you can see the restored traditional apiary of Anton Janša, widely regarded as the father of modern beekeeping. It climbs to the pretty little Church of St Peter, which hides an unexpectedly lavish cycle of frescoes by the 16th-century master Jernej of Loka, before passing through Begunje and the beautifully preserved Baroque town of Radovljica, with its beekeeping museum. From here the trail heads to the town of Bled, the most visited place in Slovenia, with

Swing bridge on the River Soča near Kobarid (Stage 13)

its beautiful lakeside setting, then up and across the remote and rugged Pokljuka plateau before descending to Stara Fužina and Lake Bohinj.

Lake Bohinj is generally seen as the gateway to Triglav and hikes in the Seven Lakes Valley – however the Juliana turns in the opposite direction, towards Bohinjska Bistrica, then up over the Vrh Bače Pass and down to Podbrdo in Baška Grapa, steep and rugged and way off the usual list of places to visit in Slovenia. From Most na Soči, the Juliana follows the Soča Valley northwest, passing through Tolmin and Kobarid, taking in relics from WW1, when this area formed part of the Isonzo Front, to reach the beautiful little town of Bovec.

Instead of following the Soča east from here, the Juliana follows the less visited Koritnica Valley, passing

the massive Kluž fortress which sits above a vertiginous gorge, to Log pod Mangartom, which sits near the head of the valley framed by the peaks of Mangart and Jalovec. Crossing the Predil Pass into Italy's Friuli-Venezia Giulia region, it passes the remote-feeling Lago del Predil, and the village of Cave del Predil, where lead and zinc were mined from at least the 13th century. Finally, after descending to Tarvisio the Juliana turns east, following a disused railway line transformed into a cycling and hiking trail, crossing back over the border into Slovenia and returning to Kranjska Gora.

An extension to the main Juliana circuit was added shortly after the trail was launched, going from Tolmin up onto the Kolovrat Ridge alongside the Italian border, and heading south across a landscape packed with

The trail through the Koritnica Valley (Stage 14)

haunting relics of WW1, through the Brda wine region, and finishing at Solkan near Nova Gorica, from where trains run back to Tolmin. Though often described as an optional extension, it should really be considered an integral part of the main route, and is a hugely rewarding addition.

A number of short detours off the Juliana are included in this guide, as recommended excursions – to the Peričnik Waterfalls, the Vintgar Gorge, the Savica Waterfall, Tolmin Gorges, Kozjak Waterfall and the Soča Gorge.

GEOGRAPHY AND GEOLOGY

The Julian Alps (*Julijske Alpe* in Slovene) form part of the Southern Limestone Alps. Named the *Alpe Iulia* by the Romans, after Julius Caesar who founded a forum (marketplace) at nearby Cividale dei Friuli, they cover an area of around 4400km^2, around two thirds of which lies in Slovenia (much of it in Triglav National Park), the other third in Italy's Friuli-Venezia Giulia province.

Their northern boundary lies along the Sava Dolinka, which runs between the Eastern Julian Alps and the Karawanke in Slovenia, and the Val Canale which divides the Western Julian Alps in Italy from the Carnic Alps. In the west they are bordered by the Friulian plain; in the east they are delineated by the Sava Bohinjka, which along with the Sava Dolinka is one of the two arms forming the River Sava. Most of the Eastern Julian Alps is

included within Triglav National Park, with the River Soča running along its western edge.

The highest peak in the Julian Alps is Triglav (2864m), Slovenia's highest mountain, followed by Jôf di Montasio (2755m) in Italy. There are numerous other peaks over 2500m including Škrlatica (2740m), Mangart (2679m), Jalovec (2645m) and Razor (2601m).

Like the other ranges of the Southern Alps, the Julian Alps were formed through the accumulation of shells and other marine life, deposited on the bed of a shallow, tropical sea on the margins of the great Tethys Ocean, over 200 million years ago. After the closing of the ocean, these deposits which had built up to a thickness of over 1000 metres were displaced and shifted northwards with the movement of the earth's crust, jumbled around and thrust upwards as a series of nappes with the collision of the European and Adriatic plates. Finally their broad valleys were scoured by vast glaciers, and deep gorges carved by rivers such as the Soča and Koritnica. Karst features abound, and the Julian Alps are pitted with caves, fissures, dolines and sinkholes – the Migovec System with its entrance near Tolmin is the longest cave system in Slovenia, at over 43km.

CLIMATE

Hardly surprisingly, the Julian Alps in Slovenia experience an Alpine climate, with cold winter and short,

Kranjska Gora (Rateče) climate

	Jan	Feb	Mar	Apr	May	Jun	Jul	Aug	Sep	Oct	Nov	Dec
Average max temp (°C)	1.6	4.6	8.6	12.4	17.9	21.3	23.8	23.1	18.5	13.6	6.6	1.6
Average min temp (°C)	-8	-7.2	-3.4	0.6	5.2	8.7	10.5	10.3	6.6	2.8	-2.1	-6.5
Mean temp (°C)	-3.9	-2.2	1.7	5.9	11.5	15	17	16.1	11.7	7.3	1.5	-2.9
Precipitation (mm)	58	57	85	107	121	141	144	151	160	164	159	111
Days with snow cover	29	25	21	7	0	0	0	0	0	1	9	25

warm summers. June, July and August are the warmest months, when you can expect average maximum temperatures of around 20 or 22°C, with the highest mean temperatures occurring in July, dropping to a minimum of around 11°C. In May and September, average maximum temperatures reach around 18°C. The Julian Alps have a higher level of precipitation than the rest of Slovenia. Rainfall is highest in October and November, but you have a good chance of some rain along the Juliana in the early summer too, and during the summer months, there is a chance of thunderstorms in the afternoons. First snowfall generally occurs anytime from late October, and sets in properly in November. January is the coldest month, when the average minimum temperature gets down to around -7°C. These are the temperatures you can expect in the Upper Sava Valley – higher up on the mountain slopes they can be considerably lower. The lowest temperature ever recorded in Slovenia was registered on Lepa Komna, a plateau west of Lake Bohinj – an eye-watering -49°C. In Rateče on the north side of the Julian Alps, the number of days per year with snow is 132; in Tolmin, down in the Soča Valley, it's just 20.

Climate data from meteo.arso. gov.si/met/en.

However, there are considerable differences in climatic conditions between different parts of the Julian Alps, due partly to the greater proximity of the Adriatic in the south-west, and obvious temperature differences between valley floors and higher ground. At Kredarica, a meteorological station on Triglav at around 2500m (so, much higher than any point on the Juliana), you can expect average maximum/minimum temperatures for July of between just 9.7°C and 4.4°C. Microclimates abound, with temperature inversions in karst depressions, and mist crawling across the surface of lakes and rivers. I have sat outside a restaurant in Log pod Mangartom in the sun while on the same day, friends experienced such appallingly heavy rainfall just a short distance away in the Soča Valley between Kobarid and Tolmin, that they had to completely abandon their hike for the day. Furthermore a marked rise in temperatures over recent years has been observed at Kredarica.

The strong north-eastern wind which is common further south in the Karst region and the Vipava Valley, known as the *bora*, isn't experienced in the Julian Alps – however you'll certainly notice it on the Brda section of the Juliana if it's blowing.

The moral of all of this is to come prepared – start hiking early in the day to avoid any potential afternoon storms, and always carry suitably warm, waterproof clothing.

For weather forecasts, see vreme. arso.gov.si/napoved/Ljubljana/graf

and type in a nearby location under *Poišči lokacijo*.

WHEN TO HIKE

The elevation of most stages along the Juliana Trail is relatively low, and the hiking season therefore reasonably long. Hiking the Juliana should be possible from April to late October, though you can expect snow to linger on higher areas and passes until June. At higher elevations on the surrounding mountains (not on the Juliana), snow cover will be heavier and the season shorter. The main hiking season runs from May to the beginning of October, which is when most mountain huts close (although having said that I've hiked parts of the trail as early as March, and as late as the end of November, both in good and at times glorious weather). Wildflowers will

Zelenci Nature Reserve after November snowfall (Stage 16)

be at their most profuse and colourful in early June, autumn colours (in particular larches) will be at their most vivid in the second half of October. The best time to see butterflies is from the end of May to mid July. Two big annual music festivals in Tolmin kick off in mid July and the first week of August, which can make it harder to find accommodation in that part of the Soča Valley at that time. Also, during Austria's huge European Bike Week (early September), the Predil and Vršič passes are a popular tour route, meaning that the Koritnica Valley will be a far cry from its usual peaceful self at this time.

WILDLIFE AND PLANTS

Slovenia's biodiversity is extraordinary, with the range of habitats in Triglav National Park and along the Juliana Trail ranging from high limestone summits and ridges to sprawling forests, river gorges, lush Alpine meadows, wetlands, karst plateaus and ancient peat bogs. There are over 7000 species of plants and animals in Triglav National Park alone.

Wildlife

Slovenia is home to all 'big three' European carnivores – Brown bear, Grey wolf and Eurasian lynx. There are between 400 and 500 brown bears (*Ursus arctos*) in Slovenia, most of them living in the dense forests of Kočevje, on the eastern side of Slovenia – though occasionally bears can be spotted in and around Triglav National Park (for example on the Pokljuka plateau), in very small numbers.

The number of Grey wolves (*Canis lupus*) in Slovenia has more than doubled in the past decade, with the population now standing at between 86 and 110 individuals at the last estimate (2019), forming 14 packs. The Lynx (*Lynx lynx*) is present in Slovenia but in extremely small numbers. The Life Lynx Project is working to bolster and preserve this population, partly by reinforcing the limited gene pool by introducing some Lynx from the Carpathians.

Along the Juliana you have a good chance of seeing Red deer (*Cervus elaphus*), Chamois (*Rubicapra rubicapra*), the majestic Alpine ibex (*Capra ibex*) and Alpine marmot (*Marmota marmota*). Fire salamanders (*Salamandra salamandra*) are a common sight especially after rain, and in areas above 700m you can see Alpine salamanders (*Salamandra atra*), smaller and black. The Green lizard (*Lacerta viridis*) is easily recognised by its large size and bright colouring.

Slovenia is home to around three quarters of all European bat species, including in the Julian Alps the Lesser horseshoe bat (*Rhinolophus hipposideros*), the Mediterranean horseshoe bat (*Rhinolophus euryale*), the Western barbastelle (*Barbastella barbastellus*) as well as less common species such as the Alpine long-eared

bat (*Plecotus macrobullaris*) and
Bechstein's bat (*Myotis bechsteinii*).

The Golden eagle (*Aquila chrysae-
tos*) nests within Triglav National
Park, in a few pairs. You can also
see Goshawk (*Accipiter gentilis*),
Honey buzzards (*Pernis apivorus*) and
Common buzzards (*Buteo buteo*).
Lammergeiers (*Gypaetus barbatus*)
and Griffon vultures (*Gyps fulvus*),
reintroduced just over the border in
Italy, are also present – huge birds,
unmistakable by their 2.3–2.8 metre
wingspan.

There are plenty of glossy black
Alpine chough (*Pyrrhocorax gracu-
lus*), and Alpine swifts (*Tachymarptis
melba*) rocketing across mountaintops
and ridges. Other species to look out
for include Alpine accentor (*Prunella
collaris*), White-winged snowfinch

*Fire Salamander (*Salamandra
salamandra*) on a trail above the Soča
Valley near Kobarid*

(*Montifringilla nivalis*), Rock thrush
(*Monticola saxatilis*) and Rock ptarmi-
gan (*Lagopus muta*). If you're lucky you
might see a Wallcreeper (*Tichodroma
muraria*) hidden among the rock faces,
or a White-throated dipper (*Cinclus
cinclus*) flitting above the water or
perched on the boulders of a fast-flow-
ing stream or river like the Soča.

Mountain forests are home to
Western capercaillie (*Tetrao urogal-
lus*), Black grouse (*Tetrao tetrix*) and
Hazel grouse (*Tetrastes bonasia*), as
well as the Ural owl (*Strix uralensis*),
the Eurasian pygmy owl (*Glaucidium
passerinum*) and Tengmalm's Owl
(*Aegolius funereus*). Forests are also

19

*Common blue (*Polyommatus icarus*) in a meadow near Plavški Rovt*

home to several species of wood-pecker – seven species within the national park, including the Black woodpecker (*Dryocopus martius*), at up to 46cm the largest of the woodpecker family in Europe, the Green (*Picus viridis*) and Great spotted woodpecker (*Dendrocopos major*), as well as the less common White-backed woodpecker (*Dendrocopos leucotos*) and Three-toed woodpecker (*Picoides tridactylus*).

There are 179 species of butterfly in Slovenia, and the Julian Alps are a particularly good place to see many of them. These include the Apollo (*Parnassius Apollo*) above 800m, Southern festoon (*Zerynthia polyxena*), Scarce swallowtail (*Iphiclides podalirius*), Green hairstreak (*Callophrys rubi*), Black-veined white (*Aporia crataegi*), Hungarian glider (*Neptis rivularis*), Stygian

ringlet (*Erebia styx*), Sooty copper (*Lycaena tityrus*) and Alpine argus (*Albulina orbitulus*). There are over 30 species of 'blues', which you'll sometimes encounter great clouds of as you walk through meadows – the Chalkhill blue (*Polyommatus coridon*) is one of the most widespread, but you can also see Chequered blue (*Scolitantides orion*) and Eastern baton blue (*Pseudophilotes vicrama*).

Plants

Almost 60% of Slovenia is forested – one of the highest proportions of any country in Europe – with the largest areas of forest lying in the east of the country, in the Kočevje region. The Julian Alps were also once more heavily forested than they appear now, however large areas were felled over the centuries to fuel the area's long history of iron smelting.

*Alpine cyclamen (*Cyclamen purpurascens*) in Baška Grapa*

Slovenia's Alpine forests are predominantly composed of beech (*Fagus sylvatica*), Norway spruce (*Picea abies*) and mountain pine (*Pinus mugo*), with larch (*Larix decidua*) at the tree-line turning a beautiful yellow-gold in the autumn. Mountain forests also contain hop-hornbeam (*Ostrya carpinifolia*), while black alder (*Alnus glutinosa*) and white willow (*Salix alba*) grow along the banks of rivers in their lower course.

Wildflower displays are spectacular in the Julian Alps, particularly in June – enough so that the mountain slopes above Lake Bohinj are host to a well-established International Wildflower Festival in late May/early June.

Wildflower species to look out for while hiking the Juliana include the Clusius' gentian (*Gentiana clusii*), Clustered bellflower (*Campanula glomerata*), Zois' bellflower (*Favratia zoysii*) with its distinctive, pinched mouths, endemic to the Eastern Alps, Mountain avens (*Dryas octopetala*), and Carnic lily (*Lilium carniolicum*) with its brightly coloured, drooping flower heads. You'll also find Alpine toadflax (*Linaria alpina*) among screes, hairy alpenrose (*Rhododendron hirsutum*), Triglav hawksbeard (*Crepis terglouensis*) and Triglav rose or Pink cinquefoil (*Potentilla nitida*), the latter connected to the popular legend of the *Zlatorog*, a mythical golden-horned chamois, while sundews and other carnivorous plants grow in the peat bogs of Pokljuka.

TRIGLAV NATIONAL PARK

Triglav National Park (*Triglavski narodni park*) is Slovenia's only national park, located in the

21

north-west of the country within the Eastern Julian Alps and covering an area of just under 840km² (that is, around 4% of the country's total land surface area). Named after Triglav, which sits at the centre of the park and at 2864m is Slovenia's highest summit, it first gained the status of a protected area back in 1924, when the Alpine Conservation Park in the Triglav Lakes Valley was established, covering an area of 1600ha (the initial proposal actually dates back to 1908). This area was expanded to 2000ha, and in 1961 it was declared a national park, with its present borders established by law in 1981. It has been a UNESCO Biosphere Reserve since 2003 (Julian Alps Biosphere Reserve), and includes three Natura 2000 sites (Julian Alps, Pokljuka Bogs, Radovna Stream). The name *Triglav* translates as 'three-headed', referring to the mountain's distinctive summit profile – although some have also ascribed it to the three-headed Slavic deity, Triglav.

HISTORY

Lying at the crossroads of trade routes between the Mediterranean and the Alps, and on the border between empires, Slovenia's history is long and incredibly rich.

From prehistory to the Romans

Evidence of human habitation in the Eastern Julian Alps stretches back at least as far as the Bronze Age, as proved by archaeological finds on the plateau of Lepa Komna, above Lake Bohinj, from around 2200BC. Further east, excavations at the large, Early Iron Age Hallstatt settlement at Most na Soči uncovered some 7000 graves, with a wealth of finds from 800–600BC, known as the Sveta Lucija Culture.

Elsewhere in Slovenia, archaeological finds go back much, much earlier – including the so-called Divje Babe flute, a pierced cave bear femur said to be the world's earliest musical instrument, found near Cerkno and dated to the Middle Palaeolithic, some 50,000–60,000 years ago.

During the fourth century BC, Celtic tribes settled along the Drava Valley, and a confederation of these tribes founded what would later, under the Romans, be known as Noricum – a territory corresponding roughly with Carinthia and northern Slovenia, and one which was incredibly rich in iron and other ores. Areas near Lake Bohinj with their rich iron ore deposits had been settled in the seventh century BC, and by the first century, iron making was flourishing here.

In the second century BC, the Julian Alps were inhabited by the Carni, who expanded southwest into the plains of Friuli, where they founded the city of Akileja. The Romans destroyed Celtic Akileja, and rebuilt it for themselves as Roman Aquileia. The Carni were allowed to remain on the Friulian plain west of the Julian Alps, and their name has endured to the present day – whence Carnic Alps, Carinthia, Carniola.

Under the Romans, Friuli became Regio X – a region which extended across the Julian Alps into central Slovenia – with Aquileia as its capital developing into a major ecclesiastical centre. The Romans took Noricum in 16BC, while the west of Slovenia became part of the province of Pannonia.

After the fall of the Roman Empire and the Hunnish invasions, the Ostrogoths founded a kingdom across what is now northern Italy and Slovenia, ruled by Theo the Great. The Ostrogoths were succeeded by the Lombards, who in turn fell to Charlemagne – and what are now Slovenia, Carinthia, Friuli and Bavaria all became part of the vast Carolingian Empire. Charlemagne took the title of the first Holy Roman Emperor in AD800.

Carniola and the Slavs

Slavic tribes had begun settling in what is now Slovenia from the sixth century onwards, and within a hundred years or so had reached the Kras region south-west of the Julian Alps. Srednja Vas near Lake Bohinj had a Slavic settlement by at least the eighth century. Some of these tribes founded a Slavic principality, known as Carniola – the core of what would one day become Slovenia, often at the mercy of the Avars – while another Slavic principality, Carantania, was established to the north, consisting of Carinthia and parts of northern Slovenia.

From the Holy Roman Empire to the House of Habsburg

The medieval history of Slovenia, along with the rest of Central Europe, is that of a succession of Duchies and principalities within the Holy Roman Empire, often passed backwards and forwards between one Bavarian overlord and another, and eventually becoming part of the vast Habsburg domains (the Habsburgs having grown to become the most powerful dynasty within the Holy Roman Empire), usually with the death of the last male heir.

Both Carniola and Carantania became Marches within the Holy Roman Empire – that is, defensive border provinces, in this case as a buffer against incursions by the Magyars – with both coming under the authority of the Duchy of Bavaria in 952. The capital of the March of Carniola was Krainburg (Kranj), and later Laibach (Ljubljana), and in 1364 it was elevated to the status of Duchy of Carniola. It became part of the Archduchy of Austria in the 15th century, and thus passed to the Habsburg Empire in 1619, of which it would remain a part until 1918.

In the early 14th century the Counts of Celje, vassals of the Habsburgs, rose to become an enormously powerful noble family, controlling castles and fiefdoms across Slovenia and beyond, including

Villach in Carinthia and Varaždin in Croatia, and Castle Kamen near Begunje. Their territories passed to the Habsburgs in the 1450s. The three gold stars on the Slovenian coat of arms are from the coat of arms of the Counts of Celje.

In 1077 the Patriarchate of Aquileia was granted temporal power, with the Patria of Aquileia becoming a powerful state within the Holy Roman Empire and expanding its boundaries and influence into areas of western Slovenia and Istria. The Counts of Gorizia became Vogts (a form of medieval governor) under the Patriarchate of Aquileia, and from their home in Gorizia became increasingly powerful, their territories including large parts of central Slovenia and Istria. Venice extinguished the Patriarchate of Aquileia in 1420, after which they controlled pockets of western

The Four Brave Men from Bohinj, who first climbed Triglav in 1778 (Stage 7)

Slovenia and the Slovenian coast, while in 1500 Gorizia passed to the Habsburgs, who now controlled the rest of Slovenia.

Increasingly oppressive taxes, forced labour and a failure of local lords to protect local peasants and farmers from Ottoman raids, led to the Slovene Peasant Revolt of 1515, which spread across a large part of Slovenia and involved some 80,000 people, until it was brutally suppressed. It had been preceded by the Carinthian Peasant Revolt in 1478, and was followed by several more uprisings against the nobility, including one in Tolmin in 1713, until widespread reforms of the working conditions for farmers under Maria Theresa in the 1770s.

The Illyrian Provinces

Napoleon extinguished the Venetian Republic in 1797, and the Holy Roman Empire in 1806, and following his defeat of Austria in 1809 he established the Illyrian Provinces from the territories ceded by Austria and Venice. With its capital at Ljubljana, it was administered as seven provinces and included Carniola, the western half of Carinthia and Istria – effectively, all of modern day Slovenia – as well as Croatia's Dalmatian coast and hinterland.

Napoleon introduced sweeping reforms across the provinces, on a social as well as an administrative level, including the separation of church from state, the introduction of a uniform tax system, compulsory military service and the French Civil Code. Slovene was introduced as a language in schools, and a university was founded in Ljubljana. The official languages of the Illyrian Provinces were French, German and Italian – and from 1811 Slovene, this being the first time it had been granted official status.

Following Napoleon's defeat at the Battle of Waterloo, Austria dissolved the Illyrian Provinces and from them created (minus Dalmatia) the Kingdom of Illyria – which lasted until 1848, when it was split into the Austrian crown lands of Carniola, Carinthia, and the Austrian Littoral. This period also marked the beginning of a national awakening in Slovenia and other areas within the Austrian Empire, where for decades local languages and culture had been suppressed.

WW1 and the Isonzo Front

During WW1 the front line between Austrian and Italian forces ran along the River Soča (*Isonzo* in Italian) in Slovenia, which became known as the Isonzo Front. It is not nearly so well known as the Western Front, yet between 1915 and 1917 it claimed over half a million lives – almost all of Italy's casualties for the entire war were sustained here, as troops fought to gain well-defended Austrian positions, and over long drawn out winters with freezing temperatures in which ill-equipped conscripts literally froze to death.

There were 12 Battles of the Isonzo, fighting over an area of almost no tactical significance. A young Ernest Hemingway, who served as a volunteer ambulance driver for the Italians until he was wounded in 1918, made the Isonzo Front the setting for his novel *A Farewell to Arms*.

Following WW1, the secret Treaty of London handed several areas, including Gorizia and the German and Slovene speaking Val Canale, to Italy. The sizeable Slovene population in these areas was subjected to Fascist persecution, and the use of the Slovene language was suppressed, encouraging many Slovenians to leave – either moving to the province of Slovenia within the newly created

Kingdom of Yugoslavia (the Kingdom of Serbs, Croats and Slovenes), or emigrating to the United States.

World War 2 and Yugoslavia

Hitler invaded Slovenia in April 1941, following which its administration was divided between Nazi Germany, Mussolini's Italy and the Fascist Independent State of Croatia. The Liberation Front of the Slovene Nation or OF (*Osvobodilna fronta*), an anti-Fascist political party, was formed a few days later, with the Slovene Partisans as its military arm. Slovenian armed resistance was supported by the Allies from 1943, and later in the war merged with Tito's National Liberation Army. Many of the Slovene Home Guard, which had supported the fascist occupation, were executed at the end of the war, while ethnic Italians fled to Italy.

The Federal People's Republic of Yugoslavia was formed in 1945, with Slovenia one of its six constituent states. Italy ceded the Slovenian littoral and Istria in 1947. Freedoms were far greater in Yugoslavia than in most other Eastern Bloc countries, in particular with Tito's break from Stalin in 1948. However opposition parties were still banned, there was no free press, and dissidents and critics of the Communist regime were imprisoned. The period was marked by heavy industrialisation.

Following Tito's death in 1980, political and economic tensions which had been suppressed within Yugoslavia intensified. In 1987 Slovenian dissidents launched a manifesto for reform of the floundering Yugoslav economy and the increasingly centralist policies of Serbia under its nationalist leader Slobodan Milošević, leading to the so-called Slovene Spring of 1988, which saw strikes and led to the formation of independent political parties.

Independence

Slovenia held its first democratic elections on 8 April 1990, after the election process had been opened to opposition parties for the first time. Following this it held a referendum – one of four of Yugoslavia's constituent republics to do so – in which an overwhelming 88% of the electorate voted for independence from Yugoslavia (over 94% of votes cast, from a 93% turnout). Slovenia declared its independence on 25 June 1991, as did Croatia. Belgrade refused to accept this declaration, and the following morning forces of the JNA (Yugoslav People's Army) were dispatched towards Slovenia.

Slovenia's war of independence from Yugoslavia was short in comparison with the breakup of the rest of Yugoslavia – it's known as the Ten-Day War – with the JNA being defeated due to careful preparation on Slovenia's part and their use of guerrilla tactics against a much larger and more well-armed force. Hostilities ended with the signing of the Brioni Accord on 7 July 1991.

Traditional painted beehives in Rateče (Stage 16)

Since the war Slovenia has emerged as a strong, stable economy, with a higher than average GDP per capita and a well-developed infrastructure, including a remarkably strong emphasis on sustainability and green policies. Slovenia joined the EU in 2004, and adopted the Euro in 2007.

GETTING TO SLOVENIA

By train

Travelling from the UK to Slovenia by rail is much more straightforward, and potentially cheaper, than most people might expect. The fastest route is by Eurostar to Paris, followed by a TGV-Lyria train to Zurich (4hrs), then a comfortable overnight sleeper train to Slovenia (11hrs), arriving in Jesenice or Bled around 07:00 or Ljubljana under 1hr later. Booking is easiest through www.thetrainline.com. Alternatively, using daytime trains, take the Eurostar to Brussels and from there to Frankfurt and Munich on fast German ICE services, then on to Villach in Austria and down to Jesenice in Slovenia. If you book the latter route through Deutsche Bahn (www.bahn.com) you have the option of breaking the journey with a 24hr stopover along the route, for no extra charge. Either way, there are no baggage fees or airport transfers involved, and you get the chance of spending a day or night in another European city along the way. You can book the Eurostar up to six months ahead, TGV-Lyria trains and Deutsch Bahn bookings up to four months ahead, and with a bit of forward planning you can get from the UK to the Juliana Trail for as little as £120 each way (daytime trains) or £150 each way (overnight train, based on a two-bed sleeper). Whichever route or combination of routes you plan, book the Eurostar portion as a return, as single journeys work out more expensive; when booking through Deutsche Bahn look for discounted *Sparpreis* fares. The most useful website for information on train travel within Europe is www. seat61.com. Travelling by train from elsewhere in Europe, Ljubljana is around 12hrs from Berlin, 6hrs from Vienna, under 5hrs from Venice and a little over 2hrs from Zagreb.

By air

Ljubljana airport (www.lju-airport. si/en) is located around 25km north-west of the Slovenian capital, near Brnik, and has direct flights to the UK (Easyjet, British Airways and Wizz Air) and plenty of other countries, including Finland (Finnair), France (Air France), Germany (Lufthansa) and Switzerland (Swiss). Shuttle buses run from outside the terminal building to the train/bus station in the centre of Ljubljana (www.lju-airport.si/en/ transport/bus). From Ljubljana, there are buses to Kranjska Gora, Bled and Nova Gorica, and trains to Jesenice (from where you can continue by bus to Kranjska Gora, Bled or elsewhere on the trail). There are also direct buses from the airport to Bled. Check timetables at www.ap-ljubljana.si/ en and https://arriva.si (for the latter,

you'll find the airport listed under Brnik/airport Ljubljana).

PUBLIC TRANSPORT IN THE JULIAN ALPS

One of the central precepts of the Juliana Trail was that as much as possible, stages should be accessible by public transport – both to encourage the use of local buses and trains, and to help keep this infrastructure alive (more hikers using local buses means those bus services are more likely to remain open, which benefits local communities as they can also continue to use these services). This is true for most, though not all stages – there are no bus services to the mountain hut on Stage 18, for example – but it certainly makes the trail easy to access, and to break the route down into smaller chunks, for those who don't want to hike it all in one go.

The main transport links covering the Juliana Trail are as follows:

Trains: The railway line between Jesenice (Stage 2) and Nova Gorica stops in Bjelska Dobrava/Vintgar (Stage 3), Bled (Stage 4), Bohinjska Bistrica (Stage 7), Podbrdo (Stage 9), Grahovo ob Bači (Stage 10), Most na Soči (Stage 11) and Solkan (Stage 20), plus several useful intermediate stops such as Hudajužna (Stage 9) and Podhom (Vintgar Gorge excursion). For train timetables in Slovenia see https://potniski.sz.si/en.

Buses: Some of the more useful bus routes for the Juliana Trail are

the services connecting the following points on the route:

- Kranjska Gora–Mojstana–Jesenice (Stages 1, 2 and 3)
- Radovljica–Bled–Bohinjska Bistrica–Ribčev Laz (Stages 4, 5, 7 and 8)
- Most na Soči–Tolmin (Stages 11 and 12)
- Tolmin–Kobarid (Stage 12)
- Cave del Predil–Tarvisio (Stage 15)

For bus timetables see www.ap-ljubljana.si/en (Ljubljana bus station, but covering routes all over the country) and https://arriva.si. During July/August there are some handy shuttle services, including to the Memorial Church of the Holy Spirit at Javorca from Tolmin, and over the Predil Pass – see www.soca-valley.com/en/soca-valley/sustainable-mobility.

Prices are very reasonable for public transport – expect to pay €1.80 for a bus ticket from Most na Soči to Tolmin, or just €3.40 for a one-way train ticket from Solkan to Most na Soči. Buy train tickets at the station (cash or card); bus tickets can be bought from the driver (cash).

ACCOMMODATION

Almost all stages on the Juliana end in small towns or villages, where you'll find guesthouses, hotels and B&Bs. There are just two exceptions, both on the Brda section, where stages end at a mountain hut. In any case, there is no need to carry sleeping bags or a tent or other camping equipment (though a lightweight sheet sleeping bag or liner may be useful in the two mountain huts) – wild camping is in

any case not allowed, and any camping at all within Triglav National Park is strictly prohibited.

There is quite a range of accommodation in larger centres such as Kranjska Gora and Bled, covering a wide range of budgets from shared rooms in hostel dorms to apartments to large hotels, while in places which see fewer visitors such as Podbrdo there may be only a small handful of places to stay – so it's advisable to book ahead.

The easiest way to book accommodation is through the Juliana Trail Booking Centre, who will book everything and send you an itinerary/accommodation vouchers, for which they'll charge a fee of 20%. If you want to stay in a particular hotel or guesthouse, make that clear (although they may not work with all accommodation providers). If you want to do the bookings yourself, it's pretty straightforward – most places can be booked online, hotels through their own website and apartments through Booking.com.

FOOD AND DRINK

Slovenian food and wine are reason enough to visit the country in themselves – and you'll have plenty of opportunities for sampling both, along the Juliana Trail. With plenty of fresh, seasonal and in many cases organic fruit and vegetables, an age-old tradition of cheese making in the lush pastures of the Julian Alps, and lots of grains grown in the lowlands of central Slovenia – not to mention wonderful honey, local game, glisteningly fresh seafood, an abundance of mushrooms and forest berries, wickedly strong fruit brandies and some extremely good wines – you can eat very, very well in Slovenia. Some traditional Slovenian dishes are included in the menu reader below – and you'll be pleased to know that stages 17–20 head down into Slovenia's best wine region.

Menu reader

- **Bohinjski mohant** A soft, crumbly, cow's milk cheese, quite tangy, made in the area around Lake Bohinj (PDO).
- **Bovški krafi** Traditional dessert from Bovec, something like giant ravioli filled with dried local tepka pears, walnuts, raisins and rum, fried in butter and breadcrumbs.
- **Bovški sir** Semi-hard sheep's cheese from the area around Bovec in the Soča Valley, made from the milk of an autochthonous local breed of sheep (PDO).
- **Čompe an skuta** Boiled potatoes with *skuta*.
- **Frika** Potato and Tolminc cheese tortilla made without any egg to bind it, traditionally served with a wedge of polenta.
- **Jota** A simple, warming stew made from potato, beans, cured pork and pickled turnip (or sometimes sauerkraut).

Traditional Tolminc cheese-maker Jani Kutin, at his organic farm (Ekološka kmetija Pri Križarju) in the small mountain settlement of Čadrg, above Tolmin

- **Kranjska klobasa** Cured pork sausage from the Gorenjska region in northern Slovenia (PGI).
- **Pohorski lonec** Stew from the Pohorje region made with buckwheat and a mixture of pork, beef and lamb.
- **Pršut** Dry-cured ham (the best comes from the Kras region and the Vipava Valley).
- **Ričet** Vegetable stew with barley and cured pork.
- **Skuta** Delicious fermented curd cheese (it's sometimes translated as cottage cheese but that is way off the mark).
- **Tolminc** Semi-hard cow's milk cheese from the high pastures around Tolmin, with at least 80% of its milk coming from a local breed of cattle (PDO).

LANGUAGE

The language spoken in Slovenia is Slovene (Slovenian), a South Slavic language related to Croatian and Serbian, though sufficiently different from those two languages that they are not mutually intelligible (Croatian and Serbian are largely indistinguishable from one another to the non-native speaker; Slovene will sound like an entirely different language). Written Slovene uses the Latin alphabet with some diacritics (ie not Cyrillic), so you'll find street signs, menus etc easy enough to read. English is spoken widely and to a very high level, at least in major cities or areas where

the local economy is based largely on tourism. For a glossary of useful words and phrases, see Appendix B.

MONEY

The currency in Slovenia is the Euro, which replaced the Slovenian tolar in 2007. Card payments are commonplace in hotels, restaurants and shops, but make sure you have some cash for bus fares etc. You'll find ATMs in larger centres such as Kranjska Gora, Bled and Tolmin, but not in small villages.

PHONES

The international dialling code for Slovenia is +386; omit the initial 0 from a local area code when calling from overseas or a non-Slovenian mobile. Mobile coverage is generally good in the mountains, although you'll obviously find a more limited signal in forests, steep valleys and gorges.

PUBLIC HOLIDAYS

The following public holidays are observed in Slovenia, meaning that on these days public transport will be restricted to a Sunday service at best, and shops will be closed. Those listed in italics are only partial holidays.

- **1 & 2 January** New Year Holiday
- **8 February** Prešren Day
- Good Friday, Easter Sunday, Easter Monday

- **27 April** Day of Uprising against the Occupation
- **1 & 2 May** Labour Day
- Whit Sunday
- **8 June** *Primož Trubar Day*
- **15 August** Feast of the Assumption of the Virgin Mary
- **17 August** *Unification of Prekmurje with Slovenia*
- **15 September** *Unification of Primorska with Slovenia*
- **23 October** *Slovenian Sports Day*
- **25 October** *Sovereignty Day*
- **31 October** Reformation Day
- **1 November** Day of Remembrance for the Dead
- **23 November** *Rudolf Maister Day*
- **25 December** Christmas Day
- **26 December** Independence and Unity Day

HIKING THE JULIANA TRAIL

Planning and stages

Officially, the route is broken up into 20 stages – 16 for the main circuit, plus

an additional 4 for the Brda section. See the route summary table. As a few of the stages are quite short (Stages 7, 11 and 19), it is also possible to combine these with the previous or following stage, and walk the Juliana in fewer days – although there are so many possible side trips (half a dozen of which are included in this guide) that you'd do better to take your time, and not rush. For those who need to break the route into two holidays, there are enough places along the route which are easy to get to with public transport that this is quite easy.

Where to start

Given that the Juliana Trail is a circuit (albeit with an additional, linear extension in the south), there are several points from which you could start – a decision which will mostly be based on access by public transport. The official stage numbering for the main circuit starts and finishes in Kranjska Gora (Stages 1–16), with the Brda section added on from Tolmin

View along the Koritnica Valley beyond Log pod Mangartom (Stage 14)

(Stages 17–20). Assuming you're arriving from northern Europe into Ljubljana, it makes sense to start in Kranjska Gora, Jesenice, Radovljica or Bled, all of which are easy to reach by train and/or bus. The question though, is when to do the Brda extension.

You can do the Brda extension mid-circuit, for example hike Stages 1–11, followed by Stages 17–20 then a train from Solkan back to Most na Soči, then hike Stages 12–16. Or, you could leave it until the end, meaning hike Stages 1–16, then take a bus from Kranjska Gora to Jesenice followed by a train to Most na Soči, walk or take a bus the short distance to Tolmin, and then hike Stages 17–20. At the end of this, you'd take the train from Solkan back to Jesenice, and head back to Ljubljana from there.

Personally, I think there's a rather nice argument for leaving the Brda part until the end – it has a slightly different character from the rest of the route, it means you finish your walk in wine country (what's not to like?), and Stage 20 makes for a suitably grand finale to the whole route. However, it does mean you'd lose part of a day getting the bus/train/bus from Kranjska Gora to Tolmin, and it breaks the continuum somewhat.

If you're arriving from Italy (for example, after flying into Trieste), it makes most sense to start from Tolmin or Most na Soči (by taking a train or bus to Nova Gorica, then the train to Most na Soči), then after walking the circuit, follow the Brda extension and get the train back into Italy from Nova Gorica. Coming from Austria, you'd arrive by train into Jesenice.

You can walk the route in either direction, clockwise or anticlockwise – though clockwise is preferred as it fits in with official route descriptions, and that is the direction described in this guide.

Trail markings

Hiking trails in Slovenia are well marked with a uniform red and white trail blazing on rocks and trees, and signposts (usually yellow or red). The Juliana Trail has its own set of trail markings, generally a yellow sign with

Juliana trail markings and stamp by Lake Bled (Stage 5)

the stage end and the Juliana logo, and JA marked on rocks and trees.

MAPS AND APPS

The Julian Alps in Slovenia are covered by a detailed set of maps (1:25,000 and 1:50,000) published by Kartografija (www.kartografija.si/karte/planinske-karte) and Sidarta (www.sidarta.si/en/category/maps), which you can pick up locally as well as in the UK – the Sidarta Julijske Alpe sheet (1:50,000) is particularly handy as it covers the whole range, including the Italian side. Kartografija also have a Triglavski narodni park sheet (1:50:000), and Sidarta have more detailed sheets for Kranjska Gora, Bohinj and Bovec/Trenta (all 1:25:000). These are the best maps to get if you want to explore further in and around Triglav National Park. Kompass (www.kompass.de) have a Julische Alpen sheet (1:75,000) which also covers the whole range. *The Juliana Trail Guidebook* published by the Julian Alps Association (available from tourist information offices for around €4) is useful for planning, although the maps are not detailed enough for navigation, and there is no route description.

The Juliana Trail app (https://julian-alps.com/en/p/juliana-trail-app-and-outdoor-active-mobile-app/54538353) available for iOS and Android in Slovene, English and German language versions) is very useful, with detailed mapping for each stage which can be downloaded for use offline. I have found the maps and gpx tracks accurate, and the app and maps take into account updates and changes to the official route. At present it only covers the main circuit (Stages 1–16) but the Brda extension (Stage 17–20) is due to be added.

WATER

Tap water in Slovenia is perfectly safe to drink, so there's no need to buy bottled water. If a source of water is

River Soča from the bridge at Log Čezsoški (Stage 13)

unsafe (such as the separate water supply for the sinks in the toilets at a mountain hut, as opposed to the sinks in the bathroom) there would normally be a sign saying *nepitna voda* (not drinking water). Springs are noted where they are found on a route and reliable. If in doubt, a Sawyer Mini Filter or LifeStraw collapsible squeeze filter weighs just a few grams and takes up almost no space in your pack.

HIKING WITH KIDS

The Juliana is a great walk to do with kids, not too difficult but still packed with excitement – stupendous river gorges, amazing wildlife, beautiful waterfalls and the occasional swing bridge – in a country with a wonderfully warm, genuine feeling of hospitality, where kids are always welcome.

LOW IMPACT HIKING

The Juliana Trail was designed to promote sustainable tourism in the Julian Alps, and to reduce overcrowding on Triglav and other disproportionately popular areas. Large numbers of visitors inevitably place a degree of strain on the environment, from trail erosion to waste management.

- Carry all litter out with you after a hike (and don't leave it at huts). Don't buy plastic bottles of mineral water – carry a refillable flask and/or pouches. Tap water in

Slovenia is fine to drink (and in the very few cases where it might not be, such as some of the taps outside a hut, there should be a sign to tell you so).

- Keep to established trails – walking on either side of a path simply widens it, destroying plant life and increasing erosion.
- Close gates behind you to prevent livestock wandering off.
- Use toilets at guesthouses and huts – it takes several months for toilet paper to fully decompose, and no one enjoys stumbling upon it during a hike.
- Use local public transport when possible.

SAFETY AND EMERGENCIES

The Juliana Trail and recommended excursions in this guide follow well-kept trails that are clearly marked, requiring no special equipment or climbing skills. Nevertheless, like anywhere else in the mountains, sudden changes in weather or a simple sprain can turn what started out as an easy walk into something much more challenging, and anyone venturing into the mountains should be aware of potential dangers, be prepared to administer basic first aid, and know how to react in an emergency.

- Leave a description of your planned routes with someone at home.
- Let someone at your accommodation, whether guesthouse or

- mountain hut, know your plans for the day.
- Check weather forecasts, and don't set off on high or exposed routes in bad or deteriorating weather.
- Always carry adequate warm and waterproof clothing.
- Always carry enough water, and food.
- Always carry sufficient navigational aids – maps, smart phone, compass, GPS – and know how to use them.
- Always carry a basic first aid kit, a torch, an emergency bag or 'space blanket', and a whistle for attracting attention.
- In cold or extreme weather, be alert to any of the symptoms of exposure or hypothermia: loss of coordination, slurred speech, numbness in hands and feet, shivering, shallow breathing or impaired vision. If hypothermia is suspected, get the victim out of the wind/rain, replace wet clothing with dry garments, keep the victim warm and give hot fluids and foods with high sugar and carbohydrate levels.
- Know the internationally recognised emergency signal: six audible or visible signs (whistle, torch etc) spaced evenly for one minute, followed by a minute's pause. (The answer is three signals per minute followed by a minute's pause.)

- Know the two signals for helicopter rescue: both arms raised above the head in a 'Y' shape meaning help needed; one arm raised above the head and one arm pointing downwards meaning help not needed.
- If you are taking out travel insurance, make sure it covers hiking (some policies don't).

Mountain rescue
Tel: 112

Slovenia has a well-established mountain rescue service, the GRZS (Društvo Gorska reševalna služba, www.grzs.si), which is formed of 17 local divisions, most of which were set up in the years following World War 2 (WW2), though some date back much earlier – Kranjsa Gora's mountain rescue service was established in 1912. Like similar services elsewhere in the world, it relies on the bravery of a few individuals – never call for mountain rescue services in anything but a genuine emergency. If you do need to call mountain rescue services, call 112 and be prepared to supply the following information:

- Your name and that of the person injured.
- Type of accident, number of people involved, urgency.
- Location of accident, including route/trail number and approximate altitude.
- Weather and trail conditions, including wind and visibility.

Emergency healthcare

UK and EU citizens are covered in the event of needing emergency health treatment in Slovenia, on production of a valid European Health Insurance Card. Following the UK's withdrawal from the EU, for UK citizens this means a UK Global Health Insurance Card (GHIC, replacing the former EHIC). For emergency medical treatment, you can go straight to the nearest accident and emergency unit; otherwise, for all non-emergencies you'll need to see a doctor first and get a referral.

Emergency telephone numbers

*   Mountain rescue 112
*   Euro-emergency number (covering emergency medical assistance, fire, and mountain rescue) 112
*   Police 113

USING THIS GUIDE

Timings

The timing given in the box preceding the route description refers to an average walking speed, and does not include breaks or stopping time at summits.

Altitudes and distances

Altitudes and distances are given in metres and kilometres throughout.

Abbreviations

North, south, east and west and intermediate compass bearings have been abbreviated N, S, E, W respectively. Left and right are abbreviated to L and R.

Maps

Routes are illustrated with maps at a scale of 1:50,000. Information on more detailed maps is given in the introduction to each walk.

Food and lodging

Some suggestions for accommodation are given at the end of each stage.

THE JULIANA TRAIL

Lake Bohinj and surroundings from the viewpoint near Koprivnik (Stage 6)

STAGE 1

Kranjska Gora to Mojstrana

Start	Kranjska Gora
Finish	Mojstrana
Distance	18.5km
Total ascent	325m
Total descent	595m
Time	6hrs
Terrain	Forest trails, some asphalt road, cycle path
Maximum altitude	970m (Srednji vrh)
Transport	Bus services run between Kranjska Gora and Jesenice, stopping at Gozd Martuljek and Mojstrana
Facilities	Many hotels, guesthouses and restaurants in Kranjska Gora; a few apartments and cafés in Gozd Martuljek; plenty of guesthouses and restaurants in Mojstrana
Variants	The Lower Martuljek Waterfall can be reached as a short detour from Gozd Martuljek. Some of the second half of this stage along the D2 cycle route can be avoided by following a forest trail above the R bank of the Sava Dolinka – however see the note of caution on this route.

An easy first stage, mostly along the valley of the Sava Dolinka but with a gentle climb to the open pastures at Srednji vrh, which command stupendous views of the Martuljek Group. The view from Srednji vrh is at its best very early in the morning, when the sun first hits the peaks on the opposite side of the valley – however this would mean a very early start from Kranjska Gora.

The Tourist Information Office in Kranjska Gora is on Kolodvorska ulica. Buses from Jesenice and Ljubljana stop on the edge of town beside Hotel Lipa. Walk W from the bus stop along Koroška ulica, then go L along Kolodvorska ulica past the Tourist Office to reach the centre of town. There's a reasonably large supermarket on Borovška cesta, opposite the Ramada Hotel, and several ATMs nearby. For information on places to stay and eat in Kranjska Gora, see Stage 16.

From the Tourist Information Office in Kranjska Gora, turn L along Kolodvorska ulica then R on Koroška ulica. Turn L just after Hotel Lipa, then at the bus stop

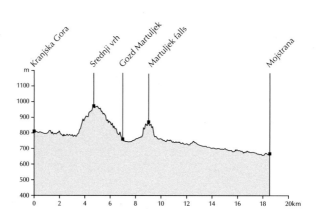

go L along an asphalted path, and R on a track towards the main road. Cross the main road (care needed, there's no pedestrian crossing and the traffic can be quite busy), then turn R along a gravel track on the far, left bank of the Sava Dolinka.

The **Sava Dolinka** rises at Zeleni vir, a beautiful wetland area W of Kranjska Gora which you'll visit on Stage 16 of the Juliana, and flows E to join the Sava Bohinjka below Radovljica, becoming the River Sava.

Bear L past a playground, then R parallel to the Sava Dolinka (not up into trees), passing behind sports grounds and keeping more or less level with the river.

View of the Martuljek Group from Srednji vrh

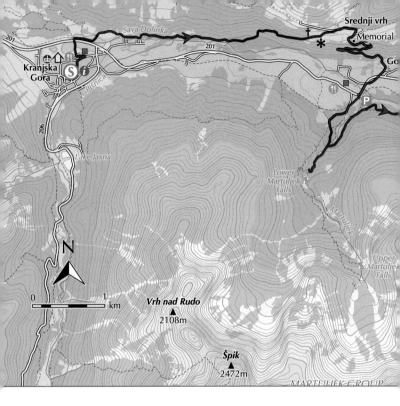

Continue on a forestry track, crossing a side stream by a small building, then bearing L and going uphill to reach the edge of a clearing at **Srednji vrh**, a little over 1hr from Kranjska Gora. Continue past a bench and a wayside shrine to a lone cottage, from where there are fabulous views of the Martuljek Group. Srednji vrh is actually the name of the hill just above the small settlement, but is applied to the area below it more generally.

The **Martuljek Group** lies between the Vrata and Krnica valleys, and the Sava Dolinka, and contains some of the most rugged, trackless wilderness anywhere in the Julian Alps. It was designated a 'landscape park' in 1949, 32 years before it was incorporated in Triglav National Park. The prominent pyramid towards the right is Špik (2472m), while the gnarled cluster at the centre (which appears lower, but is in fact higher) is made up of Velika Ponca

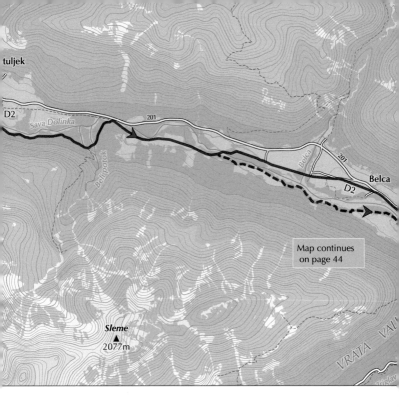

(2602m) and Veliki Oltar (2621m), and behind these (invisible from Srednji vrh) lies Škrlatica (2740m), the second highest peak in Slovenia.

Continue past the cottage to the houses of Srednji vrh (there's a gate linked to an electric fence to go through), then R along an asphalt lane, which leads gradually downhill passing a Partisan memorial on your L. The Juliana stamp for Stage 1 is here. Around 15mins from Srednji vrh, turn L onto a path through woodland skirting the edge of a small gorge carved by the Jerman river, and passing a trail descending on your L. (The trail descending L into the gorge is considerably more difficult than the Juliana, and culminates in a via ferrata for which you'd need a harness and helmet, so unless suitably equipped it's better to stick to the main trail.) After 5mins the Juliana meets the road again, which you follow downhill to reach the main road at **Gozd Martuljek**, 1hr from the cottage at Srednji vrh.

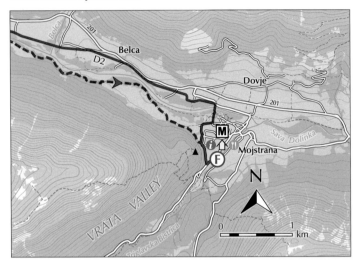

Cross the road and turn R towards the bridge and the main part of Gozd Martuljek (marked Zgornje Rute on the Juliana app mapping), passing the D2 cycle route on your L.

The **D2** is a 28km level, asphalted cycle route (also known as the Jure Robič Cycle Trail, after the late, great Slovenian cyclist) which runs between

Cyclists on the D2 trail

Kranjska Gora and Jesenice, following the course of a former railway line. The D2 makes a good, easy route for walking as well as cycling, lined by tall trees in places and crossing a bridge over the Sava Dolinka further downstream, and originally the Juliana was routed along here – though it does stay quite close to the road in places, and it can get quite busy with cyclists (and roller-bladers) at weekends. You'll rejoin the D2 later in the stage.

Cross the road bridge over the Sava Dolinka to arrive at a small parking area on your L. Go straight ahead here (ie don't follow the main road round to the R) onto a gravel track, where you'll start seeing trail markings for Slap Martuljek. Take the R fork then bear L, to reach a junction 10mins from the car park – the trail on the L is your onward route to Mojstrana, but first it's well worth making a short detour to see the Lower Martuljek waterfall, which lies just 30mins up the valley ahead of you, following the path on your R. Go R onto the Martuljek water-fall path, which hugs the base of a cliff beside the Martuljek stream, then crosses it by a wooden footbridge. It's about 20mins up to the first clear vantage point directly opposite the Lower Martuljek Waterfall (Slap Martuljek), which tumbles in a slender ribbon over a 50m cliff. (The Upper Martuljek waterfall would be a further 1hr up the path, steeper and more exposed, with an additional 250m of ascent). Descend by the same route, and turn R at the junction 10mins before the car park for the onward route to Mojstrana.

Another 10mins along the trail you'll pass a sign stating that the area has Grade 2 conservation status – an area contested with local hunting associations, which is why initially the Juliana wasn't routed this way. Bear R at a junction, following a sometimes slippery trail above the R bank of the Sava Dolinka, with some lovely glimpses of the Karavanke, and passing a hunting tower on your L. The path goes through forest then passes through a clearing and fords two strands of a small stream, the **Beli potok**. After joining a broad track, pass a large Triglav National Park sign on your R, to reach the D2, near an iron girder bridge and 75mins from the junction with the Martuljek Waterfall path.

Turn R along the D2, with views of the rocky crags of the Karavanke on your L, and after 20mins reach a farm track on your R. This provides an alternative route to Mojstana, avoiding some of the D2, however it follows official paths it hasn't officially been approved as part of the Juliana by the national park. For those who want to follow this route, follow the alternative route below; other-wise, you can continue along the D2 to Mojstana (see Main route via D2).

Alternative route

Turn R and go through an area of pasture, then take the L fork, keeping mostly level, and passing another hunting tower on your L. The trail comes closer to the river here, and becomes a little fainter after this, before bearing R on a broad clear track, to reach a bench with a lovely view of the Karavanke across the river. Continue along the path, then bear R behind factory buildings and houses, to reach an asphalt road on the edge of Mojstrana, where you rejoin the official route. Turn R along this road (Pod Grančiščem) then turn L onto Triglavska cesta to reach the Tourist Information Centre and Slovenian Mountain Museum in Mojstrana on your R.

Main route via D2

Continue straight ahead along the D2, crossing the Sava Dolinka and then the Belca stream, and coming closer to the main road, before skirting some buildings on your L, to reach a marked path on your R. Turn R onto this, crossing a footbridge and going straight across the small park, then turn R along the asphalt road beside houses. Follow this road (Ulica Alojza Rabiča, then Pod Grančiščem) around to the L, then turn L onto Triglavska cesta to reach the Tourist Information Centre and Slovenian Mountain Museum in **Mojstrana** on your R.

MOJSTRANA

One of the main gateways to Triglav National Park, Mojstrana lies at the entrance to the Vrata Valley and was founded as a mining and ironworking settlement in the 14th century, across the river from the older settlement of Dovje.

The Tourist Information Office is on Triglavska cesta, and has plenty of useful information on Triglav National Park. It's also home to the Slovenian Alpine Museum (*Slovenski planinski muzej*), with displays recounting the history of mountaineering in Slovenia. Accommodation in Mojstrana includes the excellent Aparthotel Pr' Jakapč' (Triglavska cesta 23, Tel +386 31 644 926, www.aparthotel-pr-jakapc.si), and Lukna Hostel (Triglavska cesta 15, https://www.booking.com/hotel/si/hostel-lukna.en-gb.html). Gostilna odprtih pr'Železnk (Kurirska pot 11) is a great little traditional restaurant with a terrace. There's a small supermarket near the junction of Triglavska cesta and Ulica Alojza Rabiča

Lying as it does at the entrance to the Vrata Valley, there is no shortage of excellent hiking trails to explore in the surrounding area. One thing you should definitely do while in Mojstrana is visit the Peričnik Waterfalls, only a 2hr 30min return hike away (see below).

Start/finish	Mojstrana
Distance	12km
Total ascent/descent	250m
Time	2hrs 30mins
Terrain	Gravel road, forest trail
Maximum altitude	905m (Upper Peričnik Waterfall)

A short, easy walk to one of Slovenia's most beautiful waterfalls (and there's some pretty stiff competition).

From behind the Tourist Information Office in Mojstrana, cross the footbridge over the river and turn R along the asphalt road, going straight ahead onto a track where the road turns sharply L. The track leads through forest, on the R bank of the Triglavska bistrica, sometimes opening out slightly and offering beautiful views along the river. Around 50mins from Mojstrana, cross a bridge to the opposite bank and turn L along a gravel road for a little under 10mins, to reach the Peričnik

Lower Peričnik Waterfall

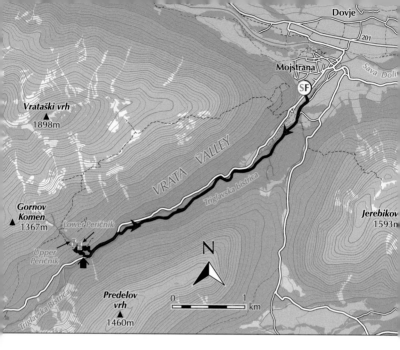

hut, Koča pri Peričniku. Turn R onto a well-signposted path opposite the hut, passing a viewpoint on your L. It's less than a 10min hike up through forest to reach the edge of a natural amphitheatre, where the **Lower Peričnik** Waterfall pours over a sheer rock wall in a 52m drop.

> The **Peričnik falls** were formed after the last Ice Age, when a glacier carved down through the pre-existing conglomerate, scouring out an impressive rock face in the process. Gradually, the power of the waterfall has eroded and undercut the softer rock below the conglomerate. The position of the waterfall has changed over time – if you look carefully, you can see notches at the top of the cliff which indicate its former positions.

Follow the path along the bottom of the cliff, which takes you behind the waterfall, to reach the other side – the view from here is even better. Avoid trying to get down closer to the pool at the bottom of the falls as the rocks are quite unstable. Then take the path on your R which ascends, steeply in places and with a flight of steel steps, to the smaller, **Upper Peričnik** Waterfall, a more modest 16m in height.

Descend to the lower falls, then staying on this side of them, follow the path (marked Koča pri Peričniku) down to the gravel road, turning L onto this to reach the Peričnik hut. Return to **Mojstrana** following your outward route.

STAGE 2
Mojstrana to Jesenice

Start	Mojstrana
Finish	Jesenice
Distance	21km
Total ascent	690m
Total descent	785m
Time	6hrs 15mins
Terrain	Gravel road, some asphalt road, forest trail
Maximum altitude	1235m
Transport	Bus services between Ljubljana and Kranjska Gora stop in Jesenice; Jesenice is on the railway line between Ljubljana and Villach. There's an infrequent bus service between Jesenice and Planina pod Golico
Facilities	A few apartments and cafés in Dovje; guesthouses and restaurants in Jesenice

Another easy stage following the valley of the Sava Dolinka, ascending slightly on its northern slopes and finishing at the usually overlooked industrial town of Jesenice, with its rich history of iron-making and mining.

From the Tourist Information Office in Mojstrana, follow Triglavska cesta NE to the edge of town, cross the Sava Dolinka and the main road, then follow the asphalt road up into the village of **Dovje**.

The village of **Dovje** is older than Mojstrana – it was a farming settlement, which is why it lies on the N, sunnier side of the valley. There are some nicely restored wooden houses – and a few rooms and apartments here, useful if everything in Mojstrana is full. You'll also pass a monument to Jakob Aljaž, who worked in Dovje for 38 years. It was Aljaž who, in 1895, purchased the

Kukova špica, a 2427m peak on the NE arm of the Martuljek Group, viewed from the trail above Dovje

summit of Triglav for a princely sum of one gold dinar, and built the small shelter there, Aljažev stup. The Juliana stamp for Stage 2 is by his memorial.

Turn R through the village, passing a shrine and bearing L where the road splits into three, then bear R, after which the asphalt peters out and you continue on a gravel road. Follow the gravel road as it leads you gradually uphill, ignoring

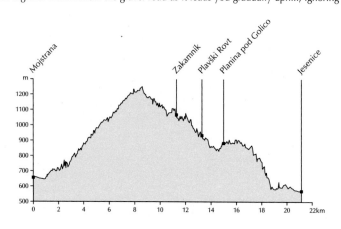

a turning on your L and a track on your R. At this point you're almost directly above the tunnel which takes the railway line between Jesenice and Villach beneath the Karavanke. Pass a meadow on your R, then another track on your R, to reach the farm buildings at **Zakamnik**, which stand on an open hillside, 3hrs from Mojstrana.

Turn R at the farm buildings and follow the gravel road downhill, passing a small memorial to Slovenian cycling legend Jure Robič – multiple winner of the men's solo Race Across America, who was killed when he was hit by a car while training on this stretch of road in 2010. The view soon opens out on your L, including a prominent wooded hill, Kogel. Follow the road down through the houses of **Plavški Rovt**, turning L onto a farm track at a roofed wooden sign. Pass Mlinski pec on your L, a huge boulder which is popular for climbing. After a rocky section pass a livestock sign, and contour the L side of a meadow below a hunting tower standing below Kogel. Go straight ahead through some houses on an asphalt road, cross the bridge over the Jesenice River to arrive in the village of **Planina pod Golico**, below two huge boulders with climbing routes.

Memorial to cyclist Jure Robič near Plavški Rovt

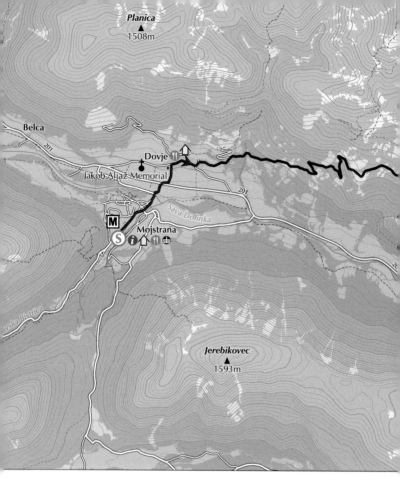

Turn R and follow the asphalt road, heading uphill and passing a shrine on your L before turning L on an asphalt road opposite a bus stop. Follow this road uphill, then go L on a track, where waymarkings for the Rudni pot (mining trail) lead you down a well maintained forest path. Go diagonally across a road passing a house and gardens, to reach a small **Chapel of St Barbara** (Sveta Barbara, the patron saint of miners) on your L.

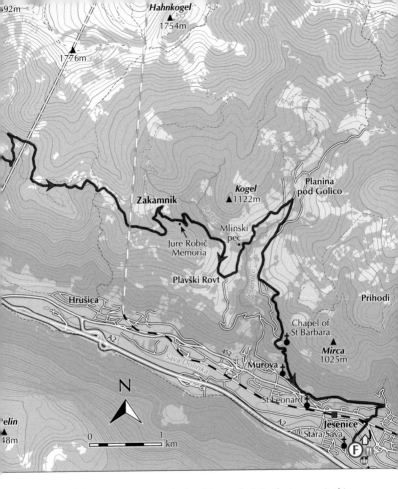

The **Rudni pot** commemorates the long history of mining for iron ore in this area, which stretches back to the 14th century. Ore was brought down to Jesenice from the mines at Planina pod Golico and elsewhere in small carts, called *žlaife* (one of them is preserved beside the chapel) and pulled by small oxen known as *terci*. The section of the route below the chapel was the steepest, so the back wheels would be removed for this section. Note the grooves carved into the rock, on the track just below the chapel – these are known as *glisani*, and were designed to provide additional traction for the carts on this steep section.

Continue downhill from the chapel, with Jesenice's industrial whir becoming audible through the trees from below. Go R where the path forks then R again, and L on a broad track, before passing a second chapel (also dedicated to St Barbara) on your R. Go onto an asphalt road, passing through **Murova**, the old miners' quarter and the earliest area of settlement in Jesenice, where some of the houses have been restored (see house #19 on your L), and passing the large, imposing **Church of St Leonard** (Crkev sv. Lenarta na Jesenicah) on your R.

The **Church of St Leonard**, which was originally dedicated to St Mary Magdalene, is first mentioned in 1460, and was later dedicated to St Leonard of Noblac (patron saint of political prisoners, among other things). Its present appearance including the striking W façade dates mainly from renovations during the 1930s, and is the work of architects Dragotin Fatur (a pupil of Slovenia's greatest architect, Jože Plečnik) and Miro Kos.

Keep uphill of the church, ascending slightly then following a gravel promenade above the town. Turn R onto an asphalt road, then L down a flight of steps, to reach the main road in **Jesenice**. Cross the road, and if you're staying at Klub Zlata Ribica, it's just on your L. To continue to the end of the stage at Stara Sava, turn R, go L over the pedestrian crossing and turn L along the main road, then R over the footbridge. Keep straight ahead across a second footbridge, pass a large shopping centre on your L to arrive at Stara Sava, the well-preserved core of the town's historic iron-making industry, with its church and manor house, on your R, beside a small park. The stamp, if you're looking for it, is in the lucky horseshoe.

JESENICE

The heart of Slovenia's historic iron-making industry, Jesenice developed at the confluence of the Sava Dolinka and the Ukova river in the 16th century. By this time, the small mountain streams further up the hillsides were no longer sufficient to support the demand of the burgeoning iron industry, and several mining settlements and foundries grew up independently on or close to the valley floor, of which Murova was the earliest, and which in the late 19th century merged into one town. Stara Sava (Old Sava, referring to the name of one of the settlements) was the heart of this new town, now beautifully restored, and complete with blast furnaces, a Baroque manor house (now home to the Slovenian Iron-making Museum www.gmj. si), worker's housing (this building, known as *Kasarna*, dates from the 18th century and was in use by ironworkers' families until the 1980s), a church (Church of Assumption of St Mary, built in 1606) and a mill.

Accommodation in Jesenice includes Klub Zlata Ribica (Cesta Toneta Tomšiča 6, Tel +386 41 691 271) which is right on the Juliana, and Guesthouse Ejga (Cesta Maršala Tita 27, www.ejga-jesenice.si) opposite the railway station. Gostilnica Chilli (Trg Toneta Čufarja 3, www.gostilnica-chilli.si) is a really good restaurant less than 50 metres from Klub Zlata Ribica, serving plenty of traditional Slovenian dishes as well as pizza. The railway station is on Cesta Maršala Tita, a 5min walk W of Gostilnica Chilli. The Tourist Information Office www.turizem.jesenice.si is also on Cesta Maršala Tita. There's a large Spar and a DM pharmacy in the shopping centre at Stara Sava.

STAGE 3
Jesenice to Begunje

Start	Jesenice
Finish	Begunje
Distance	17.5km
Total ascent	465m
Total descent	460m
Time	5hrs
Terrain	Several sections on asphalt road (one of which can easily be avoided by taking a train), forest trail, gravel road
Maximum altitude	867mm (Sankaška koča)
Transport	From Jesenice there are trains to Ljubljana and Villach (in Austria), and to Nova Gorica via Bled. Buses run from Jesenice to Kranjska Gora and Ljubljana
Facilities	A few apartments and restaurants in Žirovnica; refreshments at Sankaška koča mountain hut (weekends); guesthouses and restaurants in Begunje

An easy stage which is, historically, one of the richest sections of the Juliana – passing through Žirovnica, and the birthplace and apiary of Anton Janša in Breznica, one of the most important figures in the history of modern beekeeping. The last part of the stage takes you over a hill with wonderful views, topped with a small church with 16th-century frescoes.

However, the initial few kilometres out of Jesenice are, unavoidably, along busy main roads, with not much to commend them. My advice therefore is to skip the initial part of this stage, by taking a local train to Blejska Dobrava (the train station is actually called Vintgar), and picking up the trail from there – saving you about 90mins on busy asphalt roads, and making for a much nicer opening to this stage. You'll still have a fair bit of road walking on this stage in any case. If you do decide to hike the initial section out of Jesenice, be careful not to get caught out by an old, incorrect gpx route (since corrected on the app) or the route shown in the first edition of the Juliana booklet – the correct route stays on the L bank of the river initially, and does not cross directly from Stara Sava to the R bank.

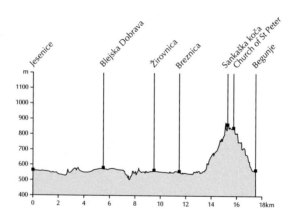

From Stara Sava, go through the car park in front of the shopping centre, cross the railway line then turn R on Fužinska cesta, then L to the roundabout. Turn R at the roundabout and follow the main road, then turn L off this and R along the much quieter Ulica Cankarjevega bataljona. Keep straight ahead at the end of

Stara Sava, Jesenice

this, still parallel to the main road, which you rejoin near a bus stop. At the next junction turn R down Cesta Janeza Finžgarja, go across the bridge to the R bank of the Sava, and follow the main road around to the L. Turn L off the main road after 10mins, at the **Lipice** bus stop, on a minor asphalt road beside houses then open fields, before bearing R up to the motorway.

Cross the bridge over the motorway (ignoring any older signs trying to send you along a gravel access road on the N side of the motorway), and follow the road straight ahead to the village of **Bjelska Dobrava**.

There is a **railway station** in the village (the station is called Vintgar, and is a useful access point for hikes to the Vintgar Gorge – see the excursion following Stage 4), and if you've skipped the initial stretch of asphalt walking, you'll start here instead. Walk SE from the station and cross the railway lines, bear L at the restaurant then turn R along an asphalt lane to rejoin the Juliana route, just beyond the edge of the village.

Just outside the village, turn L along an asphalt lane between open fields, passing hayracks, with views of Stol (2237m) and the main Karavanke ridge to the NE.

This may be one of the first of these **traditional hayracks** you've seen on the Juliana. Known as *kozolec* in Slovenian or sometimes *kazuc*, these

57

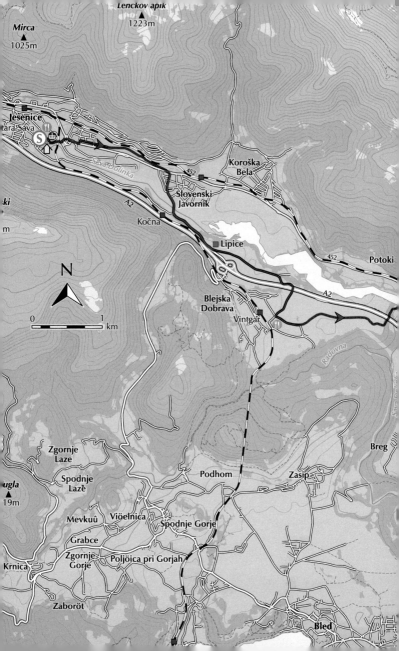

Weinasch/Vajnež
2104m

AUSTRIA

Bielschitza/Svačica
1958m

Stol
2237m

SLOVENIA

Surge Tank

Žirovnica Ⓜ

Zabreznica

Breznica

Apiary
of Anton Janša

Doslovce

Smokuški vrh
1122m

Smokuč

Rodine

Sankaška
koča

St Peter's
above Begunje

St U

ⓘ Ⓕ
Begunje
Ⓜ

Hlebce

freestanding racks for drying hay and other crops are quite different to the haystacks (hayricks) found more widely in the world (although similar structures are found in some neighbouring areas of Central Europe). You'll see plenty more of them along the Juliana, from single freestanding ones to those built in pairs or forming the lower storey of a barn.

Bear L onto a gravel road, then go downhill and under the motorway, and follow the asphalt road across the Moste Dam with views back across the dammed waters of the Sava behind you. Walk uphill into the village of **Moste**, following the road around to your R and crossing the Zavišnica stream, and passing a WW2 memorial. There are several places to eat in Žirovnica, including Gostilna Trebušnik and Gostišče Osvald.

Go through the village of **Žirovnica**, passing the 15th-century **St Martin's Church** (Crkev sv. Martina) and a small Mercator supermarket, before turning L to swing past the house where Matija Čop (1797–1835), one of Slovenia's greatest linguists and literary historians, was born. Visiting hours: www.visitzirovnica.si/en/matija-cop-birthouse-zirovnica. Return to the main road, passing a bakery and pizzeria, then a riding school on your L. You'll see a huge variety of apple trees growing in gardens beside the road here.

The rather exotic-looking building on the hill on your L as you walk through Žirovnica, is the façade of a surge tank, built for the Završnica hydroelectric power station in 1914.

Turn L past a school, up a flight of steps then R along another asphalt road. Bear L uphill, then R before a playground, then take a L fork, beside houses with well-kept, pretty gardens. Pass the large Parish Church of Our Lady of Sorrows, then at a junction turn R downhill to visit the celebrated **Apiary of Anton Janša** in Breznica.

Widely regarded as the father of modern beekeeping, **Anton Janša** was born in Breznica in 1734. Appointed by Empress Maria Theresa to teach at the

Church of St Peter above Begunje

Beekeeping School in Vienna, he wrote two pioneering books on beekeeping, made several important discoveries on the life of bees, and invented a new type of beehive. The apiary you see here is a late 19th-century replica, but shows the distinctive traditional painted panels used on beehives in Slovenia until the introduction of newer, larger hives in the 20th century. You can find out more about the long history of beekeeping in Slovenia at the Beekeeping Museum in Radovljica (Stage 4). Slovenia has the highest number of beekeepers per capita of any country in Europe, and initiated a World Bee Day in 2017, on the date of Janša's birth, 20 May.

Return to the previous junction and continue uphill, then after 10mins go L through a gate and turn R along the edge of a livestock paddock. You'll be pleased to know that you're now pretty much done with walking along asphalt roads for the day. Go uphill following a faint path, with good views when you get to the top of the rise. Keep R of the trees, over undulating pasture and passing a basketball area. Go diagonally across a farm track, heading uphill (not alongside the farm buildings), and bear L. There are no signs until you get to the top of the rise, where you'll find a well-placed bench with lovely views.

Take the L fork on the path behind the bench, heading up into the forest, contouring the hillside and gently ascending. Keep straight ahead, ignoring paths on the L and R, with the trail becoming steeper. Where a path joins from the R, go uphill on a white gravel path, keeping R where the path forks, after which it levels off slightly, to reach **Sankaška koča**, a mountain hut at 867m with a nice terrace and fabulous views (open at weekends). The Juliana stamp for Stage 3 is in front of the hut.

Follow the path R from the hut (not the track on your L) to emerge above a sloping meadow with views of the **Church of St Peter above Begunje** (Sv. Peter nad Begunjami) and the fabulous ridge of Begunjščica beyond.

The Church of St Peter above Begunje dates from the early 16th century, and the interior contains a breath-taking 16th-century fresco cycle by a local master, Jernej of Loka. These depict the Passion of Christ in 26 scenes (North Wall) and the Legend of St Peter (presbytery). Ask at the house next to the church if it's locked and you want to look at the frescoes inside (a small donation would be appropriate).

Follow the path SE from the church, heading downhill and bearing L at a junction. Take a R fork, keep R then go straight ahead at a trail junction. After descending for 30mins from the church, you emerge from the trees and go onto an asphalt lane, past houses to reach the bus stop and tourist information centre in **Begunje**, opposite Gostilna Avsenik.

BEGUNJE

Begunje (or to give it its full name, Begunje na Gorenjskem) is a small town at the entrance to the Draga Valley, below the towering ridge of Begunjščica to the N (one of the most popular and rewarding hiking routes in the area).

Kamen Castle (Grad Kamen), built in the 12th century by the Counts of Ortenburg, stands a little way outside town at the entrance to the Draga Valley. It was later owned by the Counts of Celje, and from the 15th century by the Counts of Lambergh – who abandoned the site in the 18th century and moved to the more comfortable Katzenstein Mansion. The castle ruins are well worth visiting – it's just a 1.5 kilometre walk, following the main road NE from St Ulrich's church, or follow the Lamberg Trail which leads out past the Katzenstein Mansion and contours the hillside N of the Begunjščica stream, around 2.5 kilometres. During the German occupation in WW2 Katzenstein Mansion was used as a prison, and there are several mass graves outside.

Begunje is closely associated with ski manufacture, since it was here that the ski jumping champion Rudi Finžgar founded Elan skis in 1945 (Finžgar's is a quite a story – he was drafted into the German army in WW2, escaped to join the Partisans, and began making skis for them). You can visit the Elan Alpine Ski Museum in Begunje (http://museum.elanskis.com). You can also visit the Avsenik Museum (https://www.avsenik.com) at Gostilna Avsenik – dedicated to the life and music of the hugely successful Slovenian folk musician and composer Slavko Avsenik, who was born here.

Accommodation in Begunje includes Gostilna Avsenik, also known as Gostilna Pri Jožovcu (www.avsenik.com/Gostilna-in-restavracija), Apartma Pr' Martin (www.booking.com/hotel/si/apartma-pr-martin), Apartment Murka (www.booking.com/hotel/si/apartment-murka) and Apartment Ana (www.booking.com/hotel/si/apartma-ana-begunje-na-gorenjskem). The Tourist Information Office is opposite Gostilna Pri Jožovcu.

STAGE 4
Begunje to Bled

Start	Begunje
Finish	Bled
Distance	15km
Total ascent	95m
Total descent	180m
Time	4hrs
Terrain	Paths, 4x4 tracks, and some sections on asphalt road
Maximum altitude	578m (Begunje)
Transport	Buses to Bled from Ljubljana via Radovljica; trains to Bled from Jesenice and Nova Gorica
Facilities	Plenty of hotels, guesthouses and restaurants in Bled; there are also some lovely places to stay and eat in Radovljica (1hr 45mins beyond Begunje)

Another easy stage, which is quite short, and includes a visit to the beautiful town of Radovljica, as well as finishing on the shore of iconic Lake Bled.

Walk S from Gostilna Avsenik, turning L down an asphalt lane before the cemetery. Go R at the junction then L, towards Draga and Trzic. Pass a roadside shrine

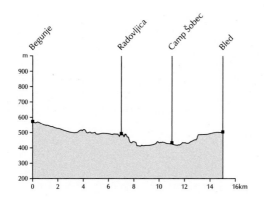

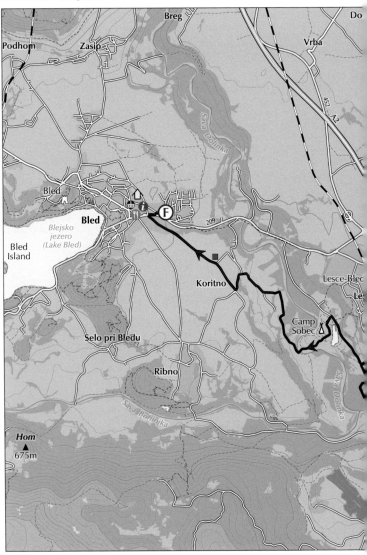

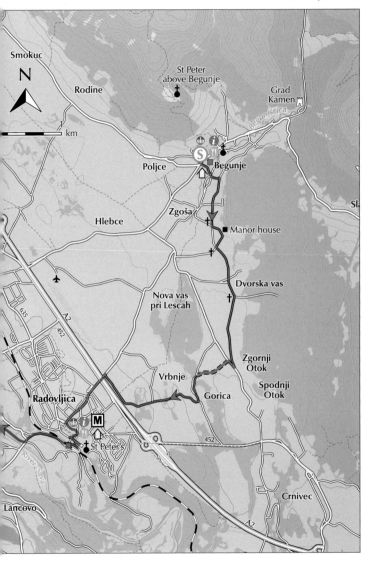

Smokuc

N

1 km

Rodine

St Peter above Begunje

Grad Kamen

Begunjščica

Poljce

Begunje

Zgoša

Manor house

Hlebce

Dvorska vas

Nova vas pri Lescah

Zgornji Otok

635

A2

452

Vrbnje

Gorica

Spodnji Otok

Radovljica

M

St Peter's

452

River Sava

Lancovo

Crnivec

A2

Sl

65

Roadside shrine between Begunje and Radovljica with Mt Stol in the distance

then bear L, passing a large manor and horse farm. Go straight ahead through the village of **Dvorska vas**, then bear R at another shrine, with views back to St Peter's Church above Begunje. Bear R at a junction (not L past a crucifix), then turn R at the village of **Zgornji Otok**, along a road initially then L on a gravel track beside cornfields then small areas of woodland. Bear R at the village of **Gorica**, then L and passing just S of the village of **Vrbnje** then R again parallel to the motorway. Go L under the motorway, then follow the road straight ahead up into **Radovljica**. Turn L along Partizanska pot beside the park and old town walls, then through the underpass and R to reach Radovljica's main square, Linhartov trg, 1hr 45mins from Begunje.

RADOVLJICA

Radovljica (also written Radol'ca) is one of the most beautiful towns on the Juliana, or anywhere in Slovenia for that matter. Its well preserved main square, Lindhartov trg, is surrounded by 16–18th-century houses, including the large Radovljica Manor. A settlement built around St Peter's Church (Cerkev sv. Petra, just beyond the far end of the square) is attested in the late 1300s, built at the request of the Patriarchs of Aquileia. Hiding within a rather nondescript late 19th-century shell, St Peter's is a three-nave Gothic

Lindhartov trg, the main square in Radovljica

church, built in the years after 1495 (see the date above the entrance portal) on the remains of an earlier church. There's some nice vaulting inside, along with an 18th-century black marble altar, and fragments of 17th-century frescoes. Don't miss the Beekeeping Museum (Čebelarski Muzej, www.mro.si/en/musem-of-apiculture) with its painted beehive panels – a unique part of Slovenian folk art – dating back to the 1700s. The Gingerbread Museum is also worth a look (www.lectar.com). There's a small shrine behind St Peter's dedicated to Edith Stein, one of the six patron saints of Europe, who was murdered at Auschwitz.

There's a very convincing argument for stopping in Radovljica for the night – accommodation includes Kunstelj (www.kunstelj.si/en), Vila Radol'ca (www.radolca.si/en/accommodation/vila-radolca), Penzion Kovec (www.booking.com/hotel/si/penzion-kovac) and 4 Seasons Apartment (www.booking.com/hotel/si/4-seasons-apartment-radovljica), while standout places to eat include Kunstelj and Hiša Linhart (www.hisalinhart.si/en).

From the SE corner of Linhartov trg, head down a side street to a viewpoint overlooking the Sava Valley, turn R and follow the road downhill. The Juliana Stamp for Stage 4 is here. Cross the railway line, following the road around to the R, go L then onto the main road again then immediately turn R onto a path. The path takes you alongside the River Sava, and through trees, emerging into open meadows where after 30mins you'll pass a **tufa spring**, its water trickling down the hillside on your R. Keep R of a hunting tower, and join a gravel road, bearing L and downhill. At the junction, go straight ahead into **Camp Sobec**. The route

Bled Castle and Lake

here isn't very clearly marked, but if you turn L after the Reception and head roughly SW to the far end of the campsite, you'll end up in Zone 7 (Sava), by a wooden footbridge. Cross the footbridge over the Sava, and turn R along a broad track, from which there are some nice views of the Karavanke, including the now familiar Begunjščica.

Turn L onto an asphalt road, up to the village of **Koritno** (where there's a bench with a fantastic view), then go R along a road past the Koritno 2 bus stop. Turn R at the main road to arrive at the Tourist Information Office in **Bled**, 2hrs from Radovljica. The town centre, with access to the lake and castle, is less than a 10min walk to the W, and is also where you'll find the bus station and most of the hotels.

BLED

Along with the lake itself, top of your list of things to see in Bled should be the castle, perched on a crag above the lake, and the small island with its church and bell tower (see Stage 5 map).

It's just a short walk uphill from the lakeside path and St Martin's church to Bled Castle (Blejski Grad, www.blejski-grad.si/en), built in the early years of the 11th century for the Bishops of Blixen, and then largely rebuilt

---

following the huge earthquake of 1511. There's a good museum inside the castle, a Baroque chapel decorated with an extensive series of 17th-century frescoes – and the views from the terrace are simply wonderful. The town of Bled below the castle grew from several medieval villages on the lakeshore.

To visit Bled Island (www.blejskiotok.si), walk along the S shore of the lake to the bay at Milno, where you can take a *pletna* – a traditional wooden boat, rowed by a standing oarsman known as a *pletnar* – over to the island. Boats leave when full (18 people) and the return journey costs €15. The title of *pletnar* was given to several families in the 18th century, and is handed down between generations. The *pletna* probably derives from a type of boat used in the Salzkammergut region in Austria, known as a *Plätten*. (You can also take an electric boat but that's really not half as fun.) Boats wait for an agreed time (usually 40mins to 1hr) at the bottom of the broad flight of stone steps leading up to a ticket office (visits cost €12) beside the church. The Church of the Mother of God (Cerkev Matere božje) was built in the 15th century, replacing an earlier church built on the site of an old pagan temple which once stood on the island – and was remodelled in Baroque style in the 17th century. The freestanding bell tower is 52m high, and it's supposed to bring good luck if you ring the bell – so up you go. As well as visiting the church and climbing the bell tower, leave time for sitting in the small café and ordering some *potica*, a traditional pastry from this part of Slovenia. The island is a popular setting for weddings (usually on a Saturday) – traditionally, the groom has to carry the bride up the flight of 99 steps if the couple wish to get married in the church.

Given that this is the most visited place in Slovenia, there's no shortage of places to stay in Bled – although having said that, its popularity means that you still need to book ahead in the summer. There's a good list of accommodation on the tourist office website www.bled.si/en/accommodation/list-of-accommodations. There's a very good restaurant in Bled Castle (www.jezersek.si/en/locations/bled-castle/bled-castle-restaurant), while down near the lake Špica (www.restavracija-spica.si) is an excellent restaurant and outstanding pizzeria, owned by former Olympic rower Jani Klemenčič.

The bus station is on Cesta Svobode, near the junction with Prešernova cesta; the railway station (Bled jezero) is at the far, NE corner of the lake, a 30min walk from the town centre. The Tourist Information Office (www.bled.si) is on Ljubljanska cesta.

SIDE TRIP
Vintgar Gorge

Start	Podhom
Finish	Zasip
Distance	5.5km
Total ascent/descent	175m
Time	1hr 50mins
Terrain	Easy path on wooden boardwalks through the gorge, 4x4 track and forest trail at the end
Maximum altitude	650m

Running 1600 metres long and 250 metres deep, the Vintgar Gorge is an exquisitely beautiful place, carved out by the River Radovna on its way to join the Sava Dolinka further N. Paths, boardwalks and bridges lead down the gorge, were the river shoots through narrows and over a succession of waterfalls, alternating with jewel-like pools and shallow, slow-moving sections, below high cliffs topped with conifers. It was opened to the public in the 1890s.

There's a ticket office at the entrance to the gorge (€10/€3 www.vintgar. si), where you can book tickets in advance (worth doing particularly in the summer). Due to the extremely large number of visitors it attracts, the Vintgar Gorge can only be walked in one direction, SW to NE (as described here) – you can't return through the gorge. At the far end of the gorge you can either follow a path then a road around via St Catherine's Church (the route described here), which has some nice views across the surrounding lowlands, and take the bus back from Zasip. Another option is to continue from the far end of the gorge to Vintgar station in Bjelska Dobrava (almost back on the route for Stage 2, but only a 1.5km walk) and get the train from there back to Bled (timetables at https://potniski.sz.si/en); or from Bjelska Dobrava follow a path above the N side of the gorge (take care not to dislodge stones) which will bring you back to the ticket office at the entrance to the gorge. To minimize crowds, go first thing in the morning, as soon as it opens – although that doesn't work well with doing this excursion on the same day as Stage 4. In any case don't try to do the walk with a full pack.

To reach the entrance of the gorge by public transport, it's easiest to take a bus to Podhom (timetables at www.arriva.si) from where it's a 25min walk to the entrance of the gorge, and take the bus back from either Podhom or Zasip. Alternatively you could walk from Bled, which is 5km from Podhom along asphalt roads.

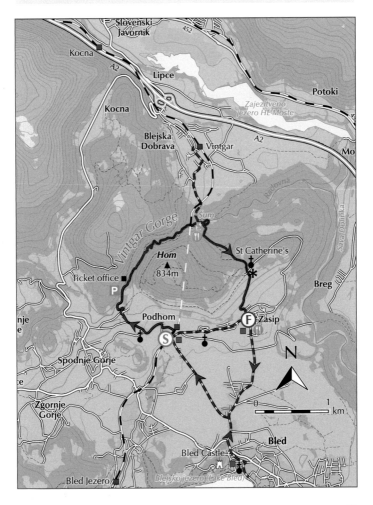

Vintgar Gorge

From the bus stop near the train station in Podhom, walk NW through the village, crossing the River Radovna and passing Gostilna Vintgar to reach the **ticket office** at the entrance to the Vintgar Gorge in 25mins. Allow a good 45mins to walk through the gorge at a leisurely pace. At the far end of the gorge, the Radovna tumbles over the 13m high Šum waterfall – it's worth crossing the footbridge and descending to the riverside, for the view of the falls. From the small café next to the Šum waterfall, follow a path SE through forest below Hom to reach **St Catherine's Church** (Cerkev sv. Katerina) in 25mins. The church dates from around 1400, and was remodelled in Baroque style in the 18th century, and there are good views out across the Sava valley from here. From the church follow the road down into **Zasip** in under 15mins, from where you can take a bus back to Bled.

STAGE 5
Bled to Goreljek na Pokljuki

Start	Bled
Finish	Hotel Sport, Goreljek na Pokljuki
Distance	21.5km
Total ascent	870m
Total descent	105m
Time	6hrs 30mins
Terrain	Good paths, 4x4 tracks, with a short initial section on asphalt road
Maximum altitude	1325m (Planina Javornik)
Transport	Buses to Bled from Ljubljana; trains to Bled from Jesenice and Most na Soči
Facilities	A few shops and cafés in the villages beyond Lake Bled, but after Krnica there no other refreshments until the end of the stage (though you might find *skuta* for sale at Planina Javornik)

This stage takes you up onto the sprawling upland plateau that is Pokljuka, an area which sees few overseas hikers despite the proximity to enormously popular Bled and Bohinj.

From the Tourist Information Office in Bled, walk W and then NW along Prešernova cesta, then bear L down to the shore of Lake Bled. Follow the lakeside promenade then the asphalt lane along its N shore, passing below the castle with some nice views across to the Bled Island. The first of the two Juliana stamps for Stage 5 is here beside the lake. At the far end of the lake, cross the road, go up a path and steps, then at **Bled jezero** (Bled railway station) turn R along a tree-lined residential street. Turn L after the garden centre, then go L at the top of the hill, over the railway line, and R on an asphalt road. Continue past houses, cross a road, and bear L uphill.

Turn L at Mercator, then L up onto an asphalt path. Pass a shrine on your L and a cemetery on your R, then the Church of St George (Cerkev sv. Jurija) on your L in the village of **Zgornje Gorje** (there's a bus stop here, and a café on the

73

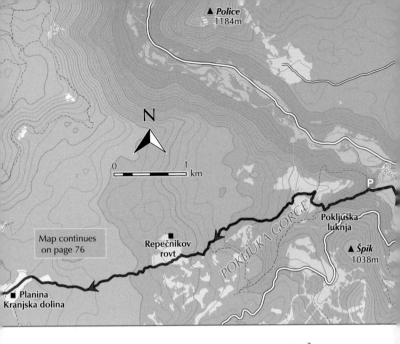

▲ **Police**
1184m

N

0   1 km

Rad...

P

Pokljuška luknja

POKLJUKA GORGE

Map continues on page 76

Repečnikov rovt ■

▲ **Špik**
1038m

■ **Planina Kranjska dolina**

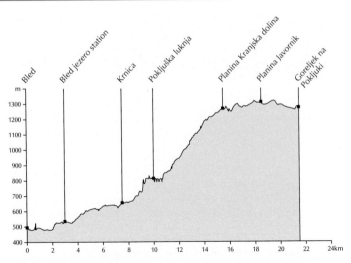

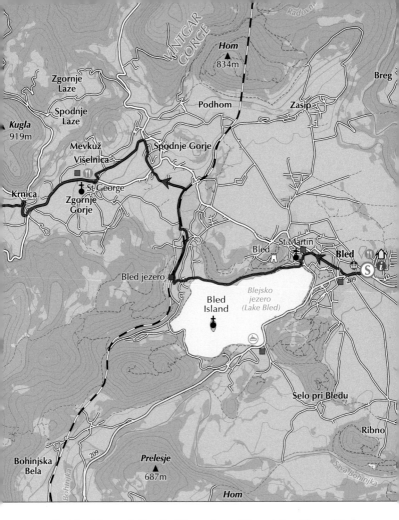

opposite side of the road). Turn R off the main road through the village of **Krnica**, and go L onto a 4x4 track after the hairpin. This leads you to a parking area on the edge of the forest, 1hr 45mins from the centre of Bled.

Bear W from the parking area, following a path which climbs gradually up a gully. This leads in 15mins up to a trail junction below a cliff, at the beginning of the dramatic rock formations of **Pokljuška luknja**.

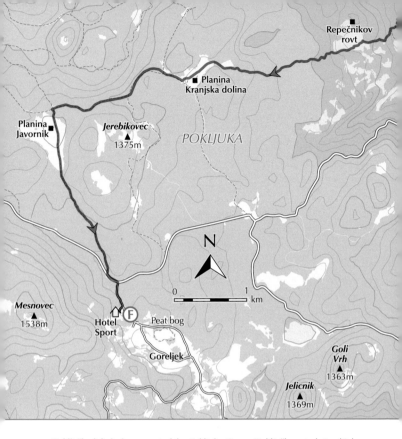

Pokljuška luknja forms part of the Pokljuka Gorge (Pokljuška soteska), which runs for around two kilometres and is 40 metres deep in places, carved by water runoff from a huge glacier some 10,000 years ago. It's possible to see more of the gorge by continuing straight ahead, a short diversion from the Juliana which leads you to galleries across cliff faces – but you'd need to return to the junction described below.

At the trail junction below a cliff, turn R and go up through the impressive rock arch. Once through this turn L, then bear R at the junction (the trail on the L is a circular route leading back to the junction below the cliff face). Go uphill and bear R, keeping the fence on your R (no trail markings), then turn L at a wooden cottage and follow a rough 4x4 track. (Ignore the trail markings on your L leading

Trail signs on the path up to Pokljuka

diagonally back through the trees.) Bear L (downhill) where the 4x4 track forks (signposted Bjelska koča), go straight ahead at the next junction, then R on a 4x4 track with the trees opening up a little ahead.

Go diagonally across a track, passing a low hill on your L. Bear L, the trail broadening into a 4x4 track then becoming a path again. Take a L fork (unmarked) to emerge at **Repečnikov rovt**, a clearing with cottages on your R, 1hr beyond Pokljuška luknja.

Walk straight ahead across one side of the clearing, through an avenue of conifers and with cottages on your R, then go uphill on a 4x4 track. Take a marked path on your R, becoming a 4x4 track, then R again on a grassy path. Turn R at a junction (unmarked), to emerge in a clearing, 40mins beyond Repečnikov rovt. This is **Planina Kranjska dolina**, a large doline and summer pasture with a handful of wooden farm buildings. Go down past the cottages then up to a broad gravel road. The second Juliana stamp for Stage 5 is on a rock beside the path. Turn R along this, passing a low hill on your L, and after 40mins go L at a junction marked Lipanca where there's a picnic table. Follow the 4x4 road through another area of open pasture – **Planina Javornik**, the highest point on this stage – passing several cottages on your R, where you might find *skuta* for sale. 30mins beyond Planina Javornik turn L onto an asphalt road, then R to follow an asphalt lane up to **Hotel Sport**.

POKLJUKA

Peat bogs on Pokljuka

Pokljuka is the most extensive high forest plateau in Triglav National Park, a great sprawl of spruce forest and mountain pastures stretching roughly 20km on each side, at an altitude of between 1100m and 1400m. Shaped by the action of the enormous Pokljuka glacier, it is especially notable for its peat bogs – among the southernmost in Europe – which are home to a fragile ecosystem and an extraordinary variety of plant species. Pokljuka was once covered with extensive beech forest, but most of this was felled to make charcoal for the iron furnaces in the region. It's a popular skiing area in winter, and hosts the World Biathlon Cup.

There are no other facilities nearby, so plan to sleep and have dinner at Hotel Sport (www.hotelpokljuka.si/en).

STAGE 6
Goreljek na Pokljuki to Stara Fužina

Start	Hotel Sport, Goreljek na Pokljuki
Finish	Stara Fužina
Distance	22km
Total ascent	330m
Total descent	1050m
Time	7hrs
Terrain	Paths and 4x4 tracks, with some asphalt roads towards the end of the stage
Maximum altitude	1285m (Goreljek)
Transport	None
Facilities	Several small guesthouses and restaurants in Stara Fužina, and larger hotels in Ribčev Laz, 30mins into Stage 7; Gostilna pri Hrvatu is a good restaurant in Srednja Vas

This is a long and beautiful descent from the Pokljuka plateau to the shores of Lake Bohinj, passing several villages, and including a truly stunning viewpoint overlooking the lake and surrounding mountains.

From Hotel Sport, return to the main road and turn R, bearing L and passing the **Chapel of St Anthony** (Kapela sv. Antona Puščavnika na Goreljeku) then turning R onto a path, through conifers to reach the edge of a large expanse of protected peat bog.

The raised **peat bogs** of Pokljuka are the remnants of former glacial lakes, formed by receding glaciers at the end of the last Ice Age. These left shallow ponds, which gradually filled with the organic remains of aquatic plants, and were later overlaid with bog mosses. Peat bogs are characterised by high levels of acidity and a low level of nutrients, conditions which have forced plant species to adapt and evolve in order to survive there – by developing extended root systems and waxy leaves to minimize water loss, for example,

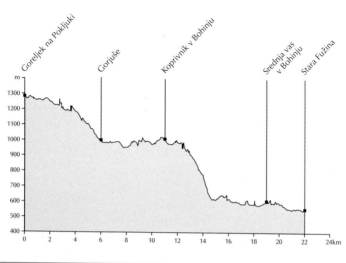

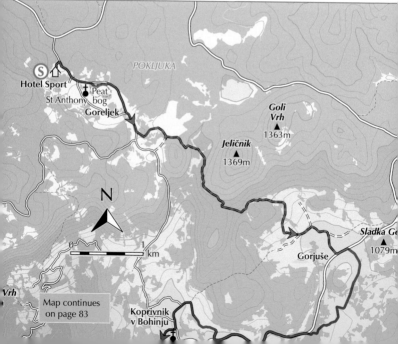

Map continues on page 83

or like the sundews and other carnivorous plants, by trapping and digesting insects.

Go L at the fence, then R onto a gravel road, to reach a junction before the village of **Goreljek**, 40mins from Hotel Sport. Go L along an asphalt road past houses, then L onto a path, behind a cottage and R onto a 4x4 track. Pass some cottages, turn R then L on a 4x4 track, passing a somewhat limited viewpoint on your R. Keep to the rough 4x4 track, ignoring trails and tracks on your L, entering an area of pasture then going onto an asphalt road at the cottages of a summer pasture, Planina Spodnji Goreljek, 1hr 50mins from Hotel Sport. Go L onto the main road, then R onto a track (not the asphalt lane next to it). Continue across open pasture, then go straight ahead down a path, and L onto an asphalt road, into the village of **Gorjuše**. Go R along an asphalt road then L, and R where the road forks, and bear L again, with a good view of the mountains on your L. Turn R onto an unmarked gravel track before two lone wooden huts, and follow this around to the L. Bear R then down to a farmhouse and an asphalt lane. Take a L fork to arrive in the village of **Koprivnik v Bohinju**, 45mins beyond Gorjuše.

Turn R at the **Church of the Exultation of the Holy Cross** (Crkev Najdenja svetega Križa), uphill on an asphalt lane then R onto a gravel track. Turn L onto a path, then R onto an asphalt lane, and a path on your R which leads around the side of a house, to reach a junction, 30mins from the church in Koprivnik

Barn with traditional hayrack near Gorjuše

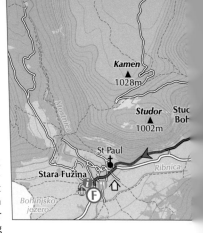

v Bohinju. Turn L here and follow the path up to the **viewpoint** and large cross in 3mins, with sweeping views over the valley ahead and Lake Bohinj. The Juliana stamp for Stage 6 is up here by the cross.

Return to the junction, turn L, and bear L keeping to a very rough 4x4 track, then turn L onto an asphalt road. Follow a well-marked path downhill, cutting across the hairpins in a series of short-cuts, and straight ahead over an asphalt lane into the village of **Jereka**. Turn R on the asphalt road, crossing a bridge over the Jereka stream, bearing L then turning R just after the prominent **Church of St Margaret** (Cerkev sv. Marjete v Jereki), which dates mostly from the 18th century – the portals are both made from green-ish tuff from Peračica, which you will have seen across the valley from Radovljica on Stage 4. (Like many rural churches it's usually not open unless there's a service or by prior arrangement.) Follow the road uphill, then go L onto a track. Cross a bridge and go straight ahead (the trail is a little unclear here, but don't go either L into the field or R up the 4x4 track), then turn R onto an asphalt road through the houses of **Bohinjska Češnjica**, and bear L. This leads gradually round to the R to arrive in **Srednja vas v Bohinju**, 1hr beyond the church in Jereka.

Standing on a slope above Srednja vas v Bohinju is the Baroque **St Martin's Church** (Cerkev sv. Martina), which has 18th-century frescoes and a Rococco-inspired organ by Johann Gottfried Kunst. Gostilna pri Hrvatu, just before the bridge over the river, is a lovely place to stop for lunch or a drink.

View across Lake Bohinj from Stara Fužina

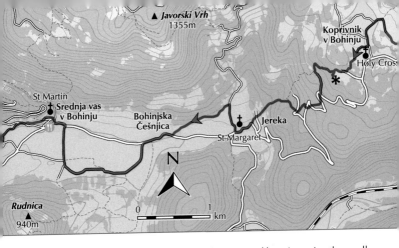

Go up past the church, then onto asphalt again, and bear L passing the small Oplen House Ethnographic Museum, and into the village of **Studor v Bohinju**. Turn R then go straight ahead onto a leafy track, then R when you reach the asphalt road beside **St Paul's Church** (Cerkev Kostel sv. Pavla). Cross the bridge and turn L, to arrive at the tourist information centre and Kulturni dom in the centre of **Stara Fužina**.

STARA FUŽINA

Stara Fužina sits just above the NE corner of Lake Bohinj, separated from the lakeshore by a broad meadow – an idyllic spot, though its name is a reference to its place in the iron industry which was once so important in this area, meaning 'old forge'. The metal shelter outside the Kulturni dom is a replica of Aljažev Stup, the shelter on the summit of Triglav. Stage 7 is quite short, leaving you plenty of time to do the recommended excursion along the shore of Lake Bohinj and up to the Savica waterfall. Another short walk which is really worth doing is to follow the River Mostnica up to its small gorge, spanned by the Devil's Bridge (Hudičev most). In any case, walk down to the lake to catch the view of the surrounding mountains in evening light.

Accommodation in Stara Fužina includes the lovely Apartments Triglav (www.apartmajitriglav.si/en) which also has a fantastic restaurant, Apartmaji Janko Rožič (www.booking.com/hotel/si/apartment-janko-rozic), Farmhouse pri Miklavu (www.booking.com/hotel/si/farmhouse-pri-miklavu) and Hike&Bike Chalets (www.hikeandbike.si/portfolio/chalet-hikebike-stara-fuzina). There are larger hotels in Ribčev Laz, 30mins into Stage 7.

SIDE TRIP
Lake Bohinj and Savica Waterfall

Start/finish	Stara Fužina
Distance	20km return
Total ascent/descent	320m
Time	4hrs 30mins
Terrain	An easy lakeside trail on broad paths and tracks, continuing along a rocky 4x4 road, and a forest path with stone steps
Maximum altitude	836m (Savica Waterfall)

This is an easy but beautiful walk along the N shore of Lake Bohinj, including a hike up to the lovely Savica waterfall. You could shorten it very slightly by getting the bus back from Ukanc to Ribčev Laz. As Stage 7 is quite short, you should have more than enough time to do this recommended side trip before continuing to Bohinjska Bistrica the same day. There's a ticket office at the start of the trail up to the Savica falls (€4/€2 in July–August, slightly less outside those months www.bohinj.si/en/savica-waterfall).

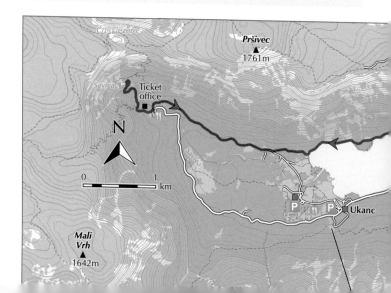

From the Tourist Information Office in Stara Fužina, walk S on the main road and turn R at the shrine, following the track down towards the lake and bearing R. Follow the broad path along the N shore of Lake Bohinj, with views of Vogel and other peaks along the watershed between the lake and the Bača and Soča valleys. Allow a little over 1hr to reach the far end of the lake, more if you get waylaid by its pleasant coves and beaches. Keep straight ahead at the W end of the lake, on a path and then a 4x4 track leading gradually uphill with the cliffs of Komarča ahead, to reach a car park, mountain hut (Koča pri Savici) and restaurant in 30mins. At the **ticket office**, go across the wooden footbridge and follow the broad, well-trodden path (with over 500 stone steps) uphill through forest, to reach a wooden shelter in 20mins, overlooking the 78m high Savica Waterfall which pours into an emerald green pool, hemmed in tightly by cliffs.

Sitting around 500m below Črno jezero, one of the lakes in the Seven Lakes Valley (a very lovely and much visited hanging valley running up towards the SW side of Triglav), the **Savica Waterfall** is fed by underground channels and subterranean lakes, and bursts from the cliff in two places, creating two separate falls. Occasionally after really heavy rain, Črno jezero overflows, and water cascades down several hundred metres of cliffs to join the Savica falls below. The falls feature in a well-known poem by Slovenia's most famous poet, France Prešeren, called *Baptism at the Savica* – and if you visit the Prešeren Monument in Ljubljana, you'll find this depicted in one of the bronze reliefs below Prešeren's statue.

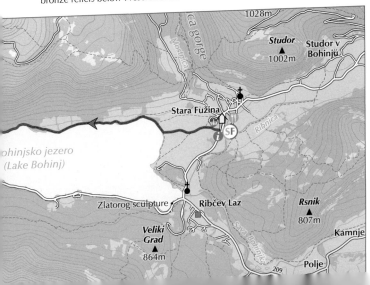

Savica Waterfall

Return to Stara Fužina by the same route.

STAGE 7
Stara Fužina to Bohinjska Bistrica

Start	Stara Fužina
Finish	Bohinjska Bistrica
Distance	11km
Total ascent	105m
Total descent	155m
Time	3hrs
Terrain	Fairly level walking on paths, 4x4 tracks and asphalt roads
Maximum altitude	592m
Transport	A bus service runs between Ribčev Laz and Bohinjska Bistrica; Boshinjska Bistrica lies on the railway line between Jesenice and Nova Gorica
Facilities	Hotels, pensions and restaurants in Ribčev Laz and Bohinjska Bistrica

This stage is quite short, meaning you should easily be able to complete it after the recommended side trip to the Savica Waterfall from Stara Fužina, or do stages 7 and 8 in the same day. Alternatively, you can continue to the village of Nemški Rovt (45mins beyond Bohinjska Bistrica), which has a nice little pension and shortens Stage 8 slightly.

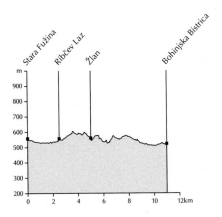

From the tourist information office in Stara Fužina, walk S along the main road then turn R at the shrine, bearing L and following a track down to the shores of Lake Bohinj.

Lake Bohinj (Bohinjsko jezero) is a long, glacial lake, hemmed in by mountains including Vogel to the SW. The Seven Lakes Valley sits above the NW corner of the lake, one of the most popular hiking areas in the Julian Alps. The lake is fed by the Savica and other streams, as well as by underground springs, and drained by the Jezernica – for a grand total of 100 metres (making it the second-shortest river in Slovenia), which after its confluence with the Mostnica becomes the Sava Bohinjka, later merging with the Sava Dolinka near Radovljica to form the Sava. During the summer the surface water temperature of Lake Bohinj gets up to around 24°C, making it a good place for a post-hike swim.

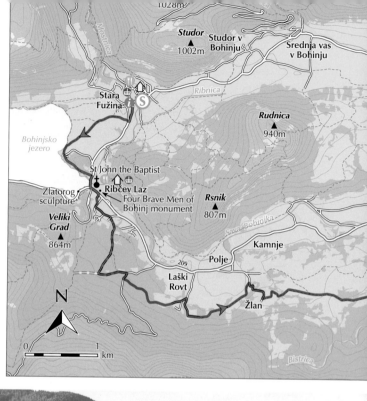

View N across Lake Bohinj from Ribčev Laz

It's worth noting that there's actually no town or village called Bohinj, it's just the name of the lake – although that is the name often used in error to describe its surroundings.

Turn L and follow the shore of the lake, before bearing L through woodland to rejoin the main road beside the bridge over the Sava Bohinjka and the Church of St John the Baptist (Crkev sv. Janeza Krstnika) at **Ribčev Laz**, 30mins from Stara Fužina – one of the most iconic views anywhere in Slovenia. For a good photo spot, follow the road W alongside the S shore of the lake for 100m or so to the small beach with a sculpture of the Zlatorog.

Cross the bridge and turn L, passing Hotel Jezero and on your L, a **monument** to the Four Brave Men from Bohinj.

The Four Brave Men from Bohinj, Ribčev Laz

The **Four Brave Men from Bohinj** were the first to successfully climb Triglav, in August 1778 – Lovrenc Willomitzer (a doctor from Stara Fužina), Štefan Rožič (a local hunter), Matija Kos (a miner from Jereka) and Luka Korošec (from Koprivnik). The expedition was encouraged and supported by Žiga (Sigmund) Zois, a scientist and patron of the arts, and a central figure of the Slovenian enlightenment. The sculpture is the work of Stojan Batič (whose sculpture of the 16th-century Peasant Revolts stands inside Ljubljana Castle), and was erected in 1978 on the 200th anniversary of the first ascent of Triglav.

Accommodation in Ribčev Laz includes the large Hotel Jezero (www.hotel-jezero.si) and Hotel Bohinj (https://hotelbohinj.si). Turn R passing the tourist information office, a Mercator and an ATM, going straight ahead onto a path, then R along an asphalt road and L at the junction. Bear R at the second fork, and go onto a gravel road towards the trees, keeping straight ahead then bearing R then turning L. Bear R and go L onto a path, then onto an asphalt lane through the houses of **Laški Rovt**. Turn R and follow the asphalt road uphill, then turn L at a junction. Go straight ahead onto a path, passing a water trough on your R, then along a gravel road, turning R onto asphalt again. Go uphill then turn L at the houses of **Žlan**, following a path down through a meadow. Go straight ahead onto an asphalt road at a junction, heading gradually downhill on a gravel track. The Juliana stamp for Stage 7 is beside the trail about 300m beyond the junction. Go straight ahead at the timber yard (not R over the bridge) and straight ahead past the next bridge (opposite Pr' Zoisove Grad), keeping to the L bank. At the next junction turn R, passing the Tomaž Godec Museum and crossing a bridge over the Bistrica. Bear L then turn R onto the main road, and R again before the roundabout, passing market stalls and a large Mercator as well as an ATM, in the centre of **Bohinjska Bistrica**, 2hrs from Ribčev Laz. Go R onto the main road then L after the car park, past the historic weighing station, cross the river and turn L to reach the railway station in under 10mins.

BOHINJSKA BISTRICA

Bohinjska Bistrica is the largest settlement in the area around Lake Bohinj, and was a major centre of the iron industry until the late 19th century, when the focus for this shifted to Jesenice. Bistrica is a common toponym in Slovenia and other countries of the former Yugoslavia, associated with rivers or springs. From Bohinjska Bistrica, the Bohinj railway line runs under 1498m Mt Kobla to Podbrdo, through a 6.3 kilometre tunnel built in 1903–1904, which is still the longest tunnel in Slovenia. During its construction, power plants were built in Bohinjska Bistrica and Podbrdo to run the drilling and ventilation equipment used to dig the tunnel. Ajdovski gradec, an Early Iron Age settlement and one of the most important archaeological sites in Slovenia, lies on a hillside just NE of the railway station – the Slovenian poet France Prešeren made it the location of one of his epic poems. To learn more about local history visit the Tomaž Godec Museum (www.bohinj.si/en/museums/tomaz-godec-museum) in the former home of local leather worker, Partisan and well-known skier, Tomaž Godec.

Accommodation includes Apartments Klemenčič (www.booking.com/hotel/si/apartments-klemencic), Alpski cvet – Apartments Gorenc (www.alpski-cvet.com/en) and Apartment Žvab (www.booking.com/hotel/si/apartma-zvab-bohinjska-bistrica). The railway station is on Triglavska cesta, just E of the Belica stream; buses stop there as well as near the roundabout. The Tourist Information Office is just N of the roundabout, on Mencingerjeva ulica. There's a large supermarket, market stalls and an ATM on Trg svobode.

STAGE 8

Bohinjska Bistrica to Podbrdo

Start	Bohinjska Bistrica
Finish	Podbrdo
Distance	14.5km
Total ascent	770
Total descent	785
Time	6hrs
Terrain	A steady climb mostly on 4x4 tracks, and a steeper descent on forest paths
Maximum altitude	1273m (Vrh Bače)
Transport	Trains from Bohinjsko Bistrica and Podbrdo to Jesenice and Nova Gorica; buses from Bohinjsko Bistrica to Stara Fužina and Bled
Facilities	A couple of places to stay and eat in Podbrdo; one guesthouse in Nemški Rovt

From the hugely popular area around Lake Bohinj, the Juliana now switches to the almost unknown (at least outside Slovenia) Bača Valley, known as Baška grapa, and crossing Vrh Bače, a pass which has some of the most breathtaking views of the entire trail. Don't be put off by brochures pointing out that you could just as well take the train under the mountains to Podbrdo to avoid a 700m climb, this is a wonderful stage, not to be missed.

From the railway station in Bohinjska Bistrica, walk S along the road then turn L under the bridge. Turn L onto the main road, past the timber yard, follow the road uphill then go R onto a path. Bear R on a 4x4 track, crossing a stream, to arrive in the village of **Nemški Rovt**, 45mins from Bohinjska Bistrica. Turn R before the **Church of St Achatius** (Cerkev sv. Ahacija), and head down to the pond and wetland area, a good spot for seeing dragonflies and marsh orchids. Pension Resje (www.penzion-resje.si) is on the E side of the village, past the church.

Go straight ahead from the pond, uphill on a rough and very steep 4x4 track into forest. Go L on a steep path, then cross a 4x4 track to arrive on the edge of open pasture by a lone bench. Follow a path along the edge of the field, then

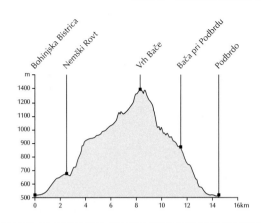

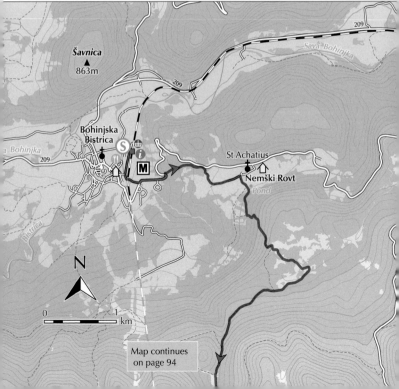

Map continues on page 94

take a path on your R, bearing L of a hunting tower, then R towards a house.
Turn R onto a broad 4x4 track, climbing steadily, and go straight ahead on a 4x4

Lookout point on Vrh Bače

track at a hairpin, then L onto a path at a bend before a cottage. This brings you to a saddle, with a parking area at the end of a 4x4 track on your L, just before emerging from the trees onto the pass, **Vrh Bače**, 2hrs from Nemški Rovt. The Juliana stamp for Stage 8 is on the sign just before the pass.

> From Vrh Bače there are **superb views** out across the Bača Valley – the mountain directly S of you is Porozen, the cliff just W of the pass is Šance, at the base of which is a bunker built in the years before WW2, part of the so-called Alpine Wall. For enhanced views, follow the path L and slightly uphill from the pass, to a narrow and exposed lookout point. There is a path (rougher and more challenging than the Juliana) following the ridge on both sides of the pass, which forms part of the Slovene Mountain Route. For centuries, the trail over Vrh Bače formed part of the trade route between the valley of the Sava Bohinjka and the Adriatic.

Go straight ahead and down from the pass, bearing R just after the small cottage (a hunter's lodge). The path is quite steep in places, rocky and narrow, but

View W from the pass at Vrh Bače

soon eases off into more comfortable switchbacks. Go straight ahead past the end of a 4x4 track, then go L onto a path, and follow a steep concrete track down into the village of **Bača pri Podbrdu**, 1hr from the pass.

Go straight ahead down a concrete track, passing the church on your R, then bear R into the trees, after which trail markings are a little scarce, and the church in Podbrdo comes into view below. Turn R at a junction, then L at the next junction, and R onto a broad gravel road, becoming asphalt. Go R onto the road past the **Church of St Nicholas** (Cerkev sv. Miklavž), and R onto the main road beside the river, in the centre of **Podbrdo**, 1hr 45mins from the pass. It's another 5mins to reach the **railway station** – go under the railway line and turn L.

PODBRDO

Podbrdo (literally, 'under the hill') has an interesting history, having been founded by settlers from Tyrol in the 16th century – Tyrolean farmers had arrived in the Bača Valley in the 13th century, at the invitation of the Patriarchs of Aquileia. These German-speaking settlers were exempt from taxes and were permitted their own mayors and language. They gradually spread to around a dozen villages, maintaining their culture and language (the South Tyrolean German dialect) well into the 19th century. Between WW1 and WW2 Podbrdo was part of the Kingdom of Italy, with a significant military presence, which didn't go down too well with the largely German-speaking population.

Accommodation in Podbrdo includes Juliana Rooms Podbrdo (www. booking.com/hotel/si/juliana-rooms-podbrdo-with-two-single-beds),

Apartment and Garden House Among the Mountains (www.booking.com/hotel/si/apartment-among-the-mountains) and Apartmaji Utrinek – at the post office (www.booking.com/hotel/si/apartmaji-utrinek-at-the-post-office). If you're unable to find anything available, your next best bet is to take the train down to Hudajužna and stay at Apartment Zver (www.apartma-zver.si), and return to Podbrdo by train in the morning. (Note that if you're taking a train from Podbrdo, it's the passenger train you want, not the one taking cars through to Most na Soči.) There's a Mercator on the main street through the centre of the town. There are a couple of places to eat – Brunarica slap, about 500 metres west of Sv. Miklavž, and Bar Baški hram next to Mercator.

STAGE 9
Podbrdo to Grahovo ob Bači

Start	Podbrdo
Finish	Grahovo ob Bači
Distance	18km
Total ascent	1110m
Total descent	1210m
Time	6hrs
Terrain	Forest paths – steep in places – with some walking on asphalt roads
Maximum altitude	998m (Kolarsko brdo)
Transport	Trains from Podbrdo and Grahovo ob Bači
Facilities	Fairly limited accommodation options in Grahovo ob Bači; in Hudajužna, 20mins off-route, there is a small guesthouse and restaurant

This stage takes you up over a pass below Črna prst, and across the N slopes of Baška grapa – steep in places and like the descent from Vrh Bače, feeling considerably more off-grid than the better known area around Lake Bohinj. If you're unable to find accommodation in Grahovo ob Bači, consider basing yourself in Podbrdo, Hudajužna or even Most na Soči for the stages in Baška grapa, and using the train to get to the start/finish of each stage.

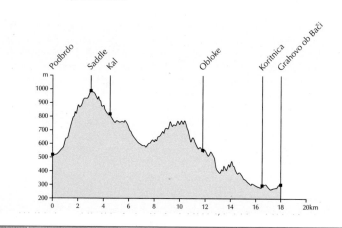

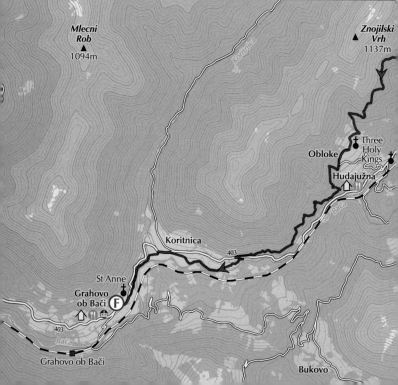

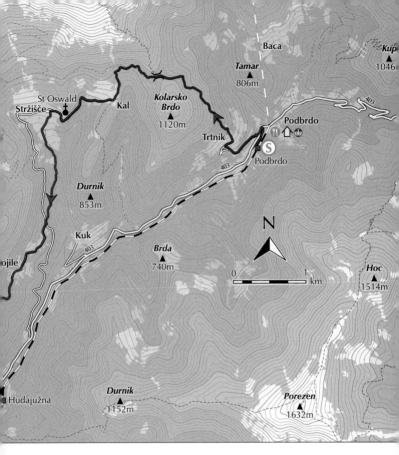

Follow the path straight ahead from the saddle, and turn R onto a 4x4 track, then bear L to arrive in the village of **Kal**, 30mins from the saddle. Go onto the asphalt road and bear R, passing **St Oswald's Church** (Cerkev sv. Ožbolt) on your R. Bear L when you reach the village of **Stržišče**, then L on an asphalt road between houses and head downhill. Bear R on a concrete track between fields, then go down a few wooden steps into a ravine, and straight ahead on a 4x4 track. Pass a ruined cottage on your L, and at the road go straight ahead up an asphalt lane. Go R up a 4x4 track just before the houses of **Znojile**, and follow a forest track uphill. The path contours steep forest slopes, before heading steeply downhill. Ignore the paths branching off on your L, then follow a concrete track

Church at Stržišče, above Baška Grapa

round to the R after a farm building and pass the Church of the Three Holy Kings (Crkev sv. Trije Kralji) in **Obloke** on your L – there are nice views from the terrace. Just after this and around 3hrs from the saddle, the road bends L, leading down to Hudajužna.

> **Hudajužna** makes a good mid-stage option if you want to stop here, with simple rooms and a restaurant (Apartment Zver www.apartma-zver.si). It's 20mins down to the village, another 5mins to the train station which is slightly further back up the valley beside the main road.

Continue straight ahead past the Hudajužna turnoff, then go L on a path beginning with an extremely steep section (slippery after rain, but not exposed), and passing a small spring running down a rock face on your R. Cross the main road and bear L down a concrete track, then go R across a field, before ascending to the main road and following this to your L into **Koritnica**. Turn L onto a path beside a house, around 50 metres before the signposted turnoff to Kamp Šorli Koritnica (the campsite is just a 5min walk N from the main road), go over a bridge and follow a track along the R bank of the River Bača. Bear R and uphill after passing a footbridge, with a view over to the 185 metre-long railway viaduct. Turn L along the main road, into **Grahovo ob Bači**, 1hr 45mins from the turnoff to Hudajužna.

On the trail above Baška Grapa

GRAHOVO OB BAČI

It's possible that the name Grahovo ob Bači (meaning Grahovo on the Bača) comes from the valley's German-speaking settlers (from the surname Grah). The Baroque Church of St Anne (Cerkev sv. Ane) above the village has frescoes inside by the Slovenian painter Zoran Mušič, one of the most celebrated Slovenian artists of the 20th century. Slovenia's first feature film with sound, *On Our Land*, was shot in Grahovo ob Bači and in neighbouring Koritnica in 1948.

Accommodation is fairly limited – there's Gostišče Brišar (www.book ing.com/hotel/si/okrepcevalnica-pri-brisarju) in the centre of the village, and Hiša Brdo Guesthouse (www.sloveniaguesthouse.eu) around one kilometre further down the road, past the turnoff to the railway station. Kamp Šorli Koritnica (www.camp-koritnica.com/en) also has one large apartment. There's a restaurant at Gostišče Brišar. To reach the railway station, continue along the main road to the far side of the village, then follow the asphalt lane down to the L – allow 15mins.

STAGE 10

Grahovo ob Bači to
Most na Soči

Start	Grahovo ob Bači
Finish	Most na Soči
Distance	19.5km
Total ascent	870m
Total descent	1020m
Time	6hrs 30mins
Terrain	Good paths and tracks, a small stream to ford (can be slippery after rain), plus a longish stretch of asphalt walking
Maximum altitude	599m (pod vrhom Senica)
Transport	Trains from Grahovo ob Bači to Most na Soči and Jesenice
Facilities	Plenty of guesthouses and apartments, and several restaurants in Most na Soči

This stage continues to follow the Bača Valley down towards the River Soča, and includes a short diversion to the incredibly beautiful Sopot Waterfall, as well as taking in some amazing views from Senica, above the confluence of the two rivers.

From the bus stop in Grahovo ob Bači go R (N) up a side-street, bearing R then L up a farm track. Bear R into a field (unclear trail markings), then pass a stone cottage, keeping to a track along the side of the field, at the edge of the forest. Go L over a wooden bridge, then R onto a 4x4 track. Go straight ahead through the houses at **Kmetija Ravence**, bear L down into the forest, then bear R before a clearing with a livestock shelter. Go through an area of mossy boulders (a good place to see salamanders), then a field. At the village of **Temljine** turn L onto an asphalt road, following this downhill past a **chapel**. Turn R onto a track, go through a gate, then L after a barn and through another gate. Zigzag down through pasture, passing several more sturdy gates, cross a shallow stream (slippery if the water level is up after heavy rain), and go straight ahead across a 4x4 track by some houses, then

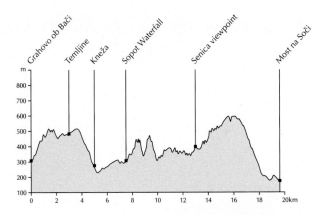

under the power lines. Follow a steep path downhill, where a sign warns of rock fall, to arrive in the village of **Kneža**, 2hrs from Grahovo ob Bači.

Turn R and follow the road through the village, crossing the river and turning L, then bearing R past the church and cemetery. Pass a trail and shrine on your L, following what will doubtless start to feel like an overly long slog on asphalt. Keep straight ahead through the village of **Podmelec**, passing the Church of the Assumption of St Mary (Cerkev sv. Marije v Podmelcu) on your L, which has frescoes inside probably from the 18th century, to arrive at a path on your R leading to the **Sopot Waterfall** (Slap Sopota), 45mins from Kneža.

Sopot Waterfall

The **Sopot Waterfall** lies just off the Juliana, and shouldn't be missed on any account. It's an easy 10min walk up

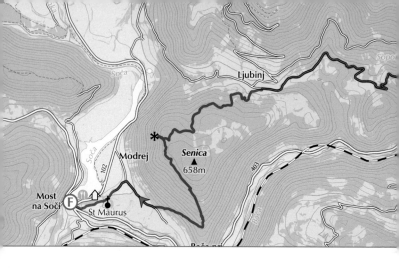

through forest, passing some benches and a spring, to arrive at the foot of the falls, where they cascade down in three stages over a 60m high cliff.

Return to the asphalt road and turn R, following it uphill through an area of sandstone outcrops. Just before the village of Ljubinj, turn L onto a 4x4 track which winds gradually up across the NW slopes of Senica. Turn R onto a marked path, which leads between boulders to a junction – go straight ahead past this to the **viewpoint** on Senica.

The **viewpoint on Senica** commands expansive views both up and down the Soča Valley, with Most na Soči on your L beyond the swollen artificial lake on the Soča at this point, and past Tolmin on your R to Mt Krn and Mt Kanin. Because of this clear view of the valley below and the ridge on the W side of the Soča, Senica was fortified by Austrian troops in WW1, although the site was never involved in any of the battles along the Isonzo Front. The Juliana stamp for Stage 10 is at the viewpoint.

Backtrack slightly to the junction and turn R, winding between more rocks, then downhill on a path and rejoining the 4x4 track briefly, to reach an asphalt lane above Modrej. Turn R and follow the road downhill, go L where the road forks and R onto a path. Pass the cemetery and **Church of St Maurus** (Cerkev sv. Mavra) on your L, descend a flight of steps, then bear R passing a church on your L, to reach the main road at a junction beside a petrol station, at the centre of **Most na Soči**.

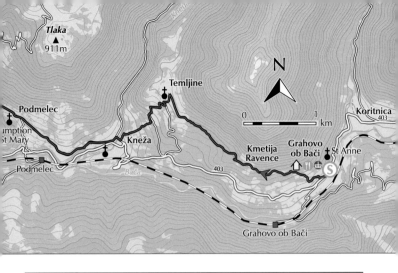

MOST NA SOČI

Most na Soči lies at the confluence of the Soča and Idrijca rivers, the former spanned by a bridge – the present one dates from the early 20th century, having replaced one from the 14th century. The adjacent lake on the Soča, a beautiful turquoise colour and a popular spot for fishing and SUPing, is artificial – created due to the presence of the nearby Doblar Hydro Plant. Until the 1950s the town was actually called Sveta Lucija (Santa Lucia) after the local church, but this was changed to Most na Soči ('Bridge on the Soča') in accordance with Yugoslavia's communist government's ruling to remove religious associations from place names.

One of the most important archaeological sites in Slovenia lies in Most na Soči. This is the large, Early Iron Age Hallstatt settlement (sixth–eighth century BC), discovered and excavated in the second half of the 19th century – including some 7000 graves, finds from which are known as the Sveta Lucija Culture and are found in museums in Vienna, Trieste and other places. The Archaeological Museum in Most na Soči (www.soca-valley.com/en/in-search-of-adventure/culture/2021012213195698/archeological-museum-most-na-soci, open by prior arrangement) includes the remains of houses from the prehistoric settlement, which once lined a street and included blacksmiths, potters and other artisans.

Accommodation in Most na Soči includes Hotel Lucija (www.hotel-lucija.com), Penzion Šterk (www.penzion-sterk.si/en), Apartmaji Taljat

Hikers descending from Senica towards Most na Soči

(www.apartma-taljat.com) and Gostišče s prenočišči pri Štefanu (www.pris-tefanu.si). Buses stop in the centre by the petrol station; the railway station is a 10min walk E from the bridge, following the main road on the R bank of the Idrijca, opposite a large WW1 monument.

STAGE 11
Most na Soči to Tolmin

Start	Most na Soči
Finish	Tolmin
Distance	8km
Total ascent	205m
Total descent	160m
Time	2hrs 30mins
Terrain	Easy walking beside and above the river, on paths with a couple of sections on asphalt
Maximum altitude	200m (Tolmin)
Transport	Trains from Most na Soči to Jesenice and Nova Gorica; buses run between Most na Soči and Tolmin
Facilities	Plenty of accommodation and restaurants in Tolmin

A short stage following the Soča upriver to Tolmin – allowing plenty of time to do the recommended side trip to the Tolmin Gorge. The route for this stage originally ran along the L bank of the Soča, however road works on that side have led to it being re-routed on the R bank. It's an equally nice route, and makes up for missing the initial riverside promenade by the fact that it's further from the main road.

Cross the bridge over the River Soča and turn R, bearing R on a slip road and following the R bank of the river upstream.

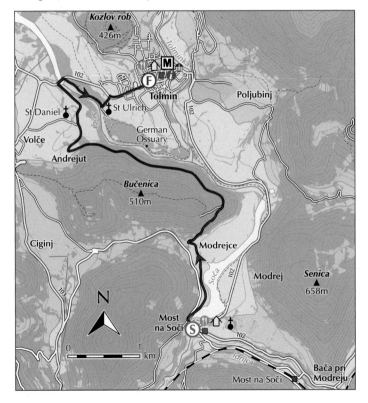

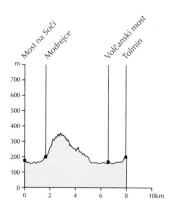

The Soča at this point swells into a **lake**, formed as a result of the first Doblar hydro plant's construction in 1939 – there are boat moorings and it's a popular place for swimming since the river slows down here, particularly on the opposite shore where there is a sheltered bay.

Go through **Modrejce**, then bear R and follow a track then a path which climbs slightly before contouring the slopes of Bučenica, which fall steeply to the river below. Pass the confluence of the Tolminka with the Soča on the opposite bank – the Tolminka is spanned by a footbridge at this point, which was the way taken by the original route for this stage. Bear R at the small settlement

River Soča between Most na Soči and Tolmin

of **Andrejut**, cross the Hotevlje stream and go onto an asphalt road, bearing R below the **Church of St Daniel** (Cerkev sv. Danijela v Volčah). The road on your L is the route you will take on Stage 17, at the beginning of the Brda extension. The church dates from the 16th century but was largely destroyed in WW1 and rebuilt, and its 16th-century frescoes by Jernej of Loka (he of the fresco cycle at St Peter's Church above Begunje on Stage 3) were lost.

Turn R and cross the bridge over the Soča (Volčanski most), then go R on a track passing a playground and a small wooden café/bar on your R. The Juliana stamp for Stage 11 is located at Volčanski most. Follow a path through woodland to the edge of the cemetery belonging to the **Church of St Ulrich** (Cerkev sv. Urh). Go L around the side of cemetery and church, and straight ahead onto the main road, passing through a pair of sculpted pillars. Follow the main road uphill towards the town centre, going straight ahead at the roundabout and cutting across a hairpin by way of a flight of steps, to reach the Tourist Information Office in **Tolmin**.

TOLMIN

Tolmin stands on a raised terrace above the confluence of the Tolminka and the Soča. The Tolmin Museum (Tolminski muzej, www.tol-muzej.si/en) is the place to start discovering more about the history and archaeology of the surrounding area. The German Ossuary down by the Soča was built in the 1930s, and holds the remains of around 1000 German soldiers killed in WW1 during the 12th Battle of the Isonzo. It's an impressive, sombre monument, made from stone imported from Südtirol, with details including gilded mosaics and a gate made from Austrian and Italian gun barrels. You can only visit the ossuary with a guide. On Kozlov rob, the green hill above Tolmin, are the rather impressive remains of a 12th century castle – it's a 30min walk up from the town on a good path.

There's plenty to see in the surrounding area, too – top of your list should be the exquisitely beautiful Church of the Holy Spirit at Javorca, built on the slopes high above the Tolminka Valley by Austrian soldiers during WW1, in memory of the fallen (a shuttle bus runs up to Javorca in the summer www.soca-valley.com/en/soca-valley/sustainable-mobility/#Tolmin, and the road is closed to all other traffic at this time), and the Tolmin Gorge, which is included as an excursion below.

One of the best-known cheeses in Slovenia, Tolminc, is produced on the high pastures above the Soča Valley around Tolmin. A semi-hard cheese, it's made primarily from milk from a local breed of cattle, and has protected designation of origin (PDO) status.

Accommodation in Tolmin includes Hotel Dvorec (www.hoteldvorec. com), Apartma Ada (www.booking.com/hotel/si/apartma-ada-tolmin), Apartment Soča Tolmin (www.booking.com/hotel/si/apartment-soca-tolmin) and Rooms pr Zajčku (www.booking.com/hotel/si/rooms-pr-zajcku). There's a useful accommodation list on the Soča Valley Tourism website www.soca-valley.com/en/accommodation, and Camp Gabrje (www.camp-gabrje.com) a short way into Stage 12. There are plenty of places to eat in the town centre, and if you don't mind a bit more of a walk, Okrepčevalica Tolminska Korita (www.tolminska-korita.si) on the path out to the Tolmin Gorge is excellent. Finally, bear in mind that there are several large music festivals in and around Tolmin in the summer, at which time most accommodation gets booked up so it pays to book well ahead. The Tourist Information Office is on Mestni trg.

SIDE TRIP
Tolmin Gorges

Start/finish	Tolmin
Distance	7.5km
Total ascent/descent	215m
Time	2hrs
Terrain	Easy walking on good paths, narrow but fenced in the gorge
Maximum altitude	306m

In a country with no shortage of jaw-droppingly beautiful gorges and waterfalls, the Tolmin Gorges (Tolminska korita) really are among the most impressive – a beautiful spot, with rushing streams and falls (and hanging rocks) all hemmed in by mossy cliffs and boulders. The name applies to two gorges, formed at the confluence of the Tolminka and Zadlaščica streams, and it also marks the lowest altitude of any point within Triglav National Park. There's a ticket office just before the entrance to the gorge itself (€8/€4 www.soca-valley.com/en/attraction/tolmin-gorges). You should easily be able to combine this excursion with the short walk from Most na Soči. There are some short tunnels and narrow paths in the gorges themselves, so it's best to go without full packs.

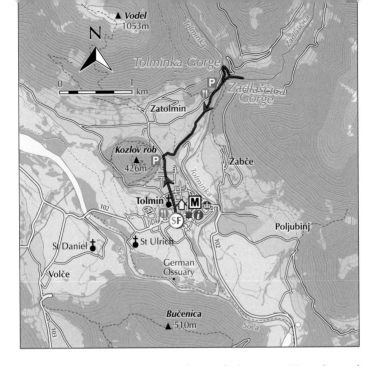

From the tourist information centre in Tolmin, walk along Gregorčičeva ulica, and turn R at the car park (about 500 metres before Zatolmin), from where a clearly marked trail heads towards the gorges, above the R bank of the Tolminka stream. Pass Okrepčevalica Tolminska Korita on your L (a good restaurant if you want to stop for lunch at some point), to reach the ticket office for the Tolmin Gorges beyond the car park.

From the ticket office, follow the path down to the right, and cross the bridge over the Tolminka, just beyond its confluence with the Zadlaščica. Turn L beside the Tolminka, going through a tunnel below the high cliffs of the Tolminka Gorge, with the river rushing below. Retrace your steps to the confluence, and cross the bridge over the Zadlaščica – the view from the other side is good, although you can't get any further along the path on this side. Recross to the R bank of the Zadlaščica, turn R and follow the path uphill, passing a trail on your L up to the road (which you'll take later) to reach a viewing platform above the Zadlaščica Gorge, with a good view of the Bear's Head (Medvedova glava), an enormous wedge of rock balanced above the river. Return to the previous junction, turn R and follow a path up to the road. Turn L along the road, crossing the so-called

Tolmin Gorges

Devil's Bridge (Hudov most), with a breathtaking view down into the narrow gorge below, then follow the road to the ticket office.

Return to Tolmin by the same route.

STAGE 12
Tolmin to Kobarid

Start	Tolmin
Finish	Kobarid
Distance	17km
Total ascent	125m
Total descent	80m
Time	4hrs
Terrain	Fairly level walking, which includes several extended stretches on asphalt roads
Maximum altitude	243m (Sv. Lovrenc)
Transport	Buses from Tolmin S; limited bus services between Tolmin and Kobarid
Facilities	Plenty of options in Kobarid, from cafés to the highest rated restaurant in Slovenia

From Tolmin, the Juliana continues up the Soča Valley with many more reminders of the fighting along the Isonzo Front during WW1, to Kobarid, another small town with plenty to see in the surrounding area.

It's difficult to avoid the road walking on this stage, since local bus services are skeletal to say the least – there's a bus departing Tolmin at 14:30, going through Volarje and Kamno to Kobarid (www.nomago.si). One way to avoid the extended stretch of asphalt walking on this stage, would be to head up to the Italian military chapel on Mt Planinica on the E side of the valley, following the Alpe Adria Trail from Gabrje, and on to the village of Drežnica, from where you can descend to Kobarid – but it's a considerably longer route, with an additional 1000m of ascent/descent.

From the tourist information office in Tolmin, follow the main road downhill and turn R at the roundabout. Pass a Mercator supermarket, and go L past the cart-racing track, then R onto a dark gravel track across fields, a route shared with the Alpe Adria Trail. Go L at the dog-training centre, then take a path on the R, becoming a 4x4 track and passing Camp Gabrje on your L. Keep straight ahead

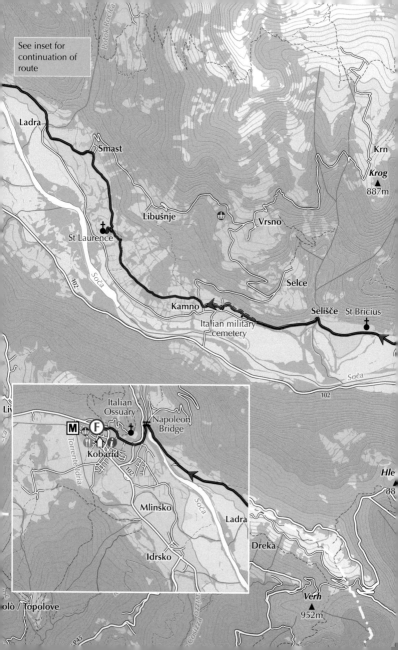

See inset for
continuation of
route

Potok Roča

Ladra

Smast

Krn
Krog
887m

Libušnje

Vrsno

St Laurence

102

Soča

Selce

Kamno

Italian military
cemetery

Selišče
St Bricius

Soča

102

Liv

Italian
Ossuary

Napoleon
Bridge

Hle
88

M F

Torrente Idria

Kobarid

102

Soča

Ladra

Mlinsko

Dreka

Idrsko

COSTA D'OZZINI

Verh
952m

olò / Topolove

P45

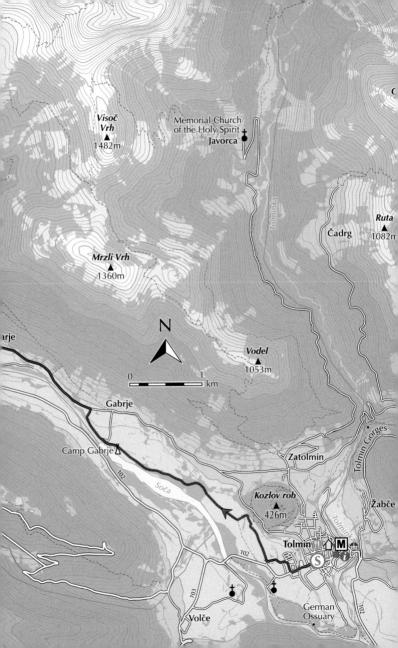

Visoč
Vrh
▲
1482m

Memorial Church
of the Holy Spirit
Javorca ♦

Tolminka

Čadrg

Ruta
1082m

Mrzli Vrh
▲
1360m

N

Vodel
▲
1053m

0   1
|————————————| km

...arje

Gabrje

Camp Gabrje ⊿

Soča

102

Zatolmin

Tolmin Gorges

Žabče

Kozlov rob
▲
426m

Tolminka

102

Tolmin 🏛 Ⓜ ℹ
Ⓢ

♦

♦

German
Ossuary

103

Volče

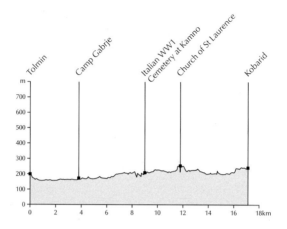

past a road on your R (the route of the Alpe Adria Trail), then bear R to reach the asphalt road, and turn L along this.

So begins one of the longer asphalt sections on the Juliana, one which in my opinion was less necessary to include on the trail than the one near Jesenice. Go through the village of **Volarje**, passing a road to Camp Vili on your L, then the

Juliana Trail between Kamno and sv. Lovrenc

Beehives beside the trail near sv. Lovrenc

Church of St Bricius (Cerkev sv. Bric), then through the village of **Selišče**, crossing the bridge over the Volarje stream. Turn R onto a 4x4 track before Kamno, passing a former Italian military cemetery on your L.

Turn L down an asphalt road, then turn R onto a 4x4 track rather than continuing into the centre of Kamno. Go R at the junction, then L along a walled, mossy path. Cross a small stream at a shallow ford, and go straight ahead on a concrete track. 40mins from the Italian military cemetery, turn L and follow the road up to the hilltop **Church of St Laurence** (Cerkev sv. Lovrenc).

The **cemetery** includes the grave of the 19th-century Slovene lyrical poet and priest Simon Gregorčič (1844–1906), who was a vicar in Kobarid and founded a reading room there. The Juliana stamp for Stage 12 is also beside the church.

Descend to the road, and continue following this through the villages of **Smast** and **Ladra**. In Ladra there's an Italian Military Chapel, consecrated in 1917 and designed by the prominent Italian architect Giovanni Michelucci, who built the Santa Maria Novella railway station in Florence. Cross the **Napoleon Bridge** over the Soča, and follow the road around to the L and uphill into the centre of **Kobarid**.

KOBARID

Kobarid lies above the R bank of the Soča, where the river narrows below the long, tapering snout of Mt Stol. The town saw heavy fighting during the Twelth Battle of the Isonzo, with much of it being destroyed.

The Kobarid Museum (Kobariški muzej, www.kobariski-muzej.si/en) is excellent, and the best place to find more information on the WW1 sites along the Isonzo (Soča) Front as well as the epic Walk of Peace (Pot Miro), which links many of these sites in a spectacular 500km long-distance trail. Just above the N edge of town, the Italian Ossuary is a deeply poignant monument housing the remains of over 7000 Italian soldiers who fell on the Soča Front. The Italian Ossuary forms part of the Kobarid Historical Trail, included as part of the recommended excursion below. The exceptionally beautiful Kozjak Waterfall is hidden up a short side valley, on the opposite bank of the Soča, and this is also included in the recommended excursion from Kobarid.

To the W of Kobarid, the Nadiža Valley stretches up to the Italian border, below Mt Stol. A hiking trail leads up Breginj, a village which was severely damaged in the 1976 Friuli earthquake, since when its small fortified cluster of old houses has been carefully restored. From there it leads up to Mt Stol, and back down its spine to Kobarid – a two day circuit, which is included as a potential side trip in some of the more recent information on the Juliana.

Accommodation in Kobarid includes the excellent Hotel Hvala and Restaurant Topli Val (www.hotelhvala.si), Apartments Masera (www.book ing.com/hotel/si/apartments-masera) which is also very good, Apartments pri nas (www.booking.com/hotel/si/apartments-pri-nas) and Kamp Koren just across the river which has wooden chalets (www.kamp-koren.si). Just W of Kobarid in the village of Staro selo, is the two-Michelin-starred 'Hiša Franko'. The Tourist Information Office is on Trg svobode.

SIDE TRIP
Kozjak Waterfall and the
Kobarid Historical Trail

Start/finish	Kobarid
Distance	9km
Total ascent/descent	285m
Time	3hrs
Terrain	Good paths beside the Soča and up to the waterfall, with some boulder hopping and wooden boardwalks at the end; a steep rocky trail up to Stari grad for the Historical Trail, followed by easy forest paths.
Maximum altitude	412m (Tonocov grad)

This is really two excursions from Kobarid combined into one circular trail – the exquisitely beautiful Kozjak Waterfall, and the Kobarid Historical Trail which takes in relics from WW1, including the site of the old castle Tonocov grad, and the Italian Ossuary.

The Kozjak Waterfall trail is very popular, and the boardwalks at the end can get quite crowded in the summer, so set off early in the morning, or if you're combining this excursion with Stage 12 you could walk it in reverse, to arrive at Kozjak later in the afternoon. There's a ticket office beside the trail just before the Kozjak falls (€5/€3 www.soca-valley.com/en/in-search-of-adventure). If you just want to walk to the waterfall and return by the same path, it's just 90mins return from Kobarid – or you could visit it at the beginning of Stage 13, in which case it's just a short detour of 25mins each way (but if it's busy you'll find the boardwalks a bit cramped for carrying a full pack).

From the Kobarid Museum, walk down to the Soča, cross the **Napoleon Bridge** and turn L. Go past the turnoff to Camp Koren, then go L onto a 4x4 road passing a lone eco-toilet on your R. Follow a broad track above the river, passing the swing bridge (which you'll cross later), then turning R onto a path just before the Kozjak stream. It's about 25mins up to the falls, crossing a bridge over the stream at a waterfall and passing the ticket office, before the path narrows, crossing boulders and a small footbridge to gain the wooden boardwalks which lead around

Kozjak Waterfall

into the canyon, where the 15m high **Kozjak Waterfall** gushes into a pool, surrounded by overhanging rock faces dripping with water.

Return to the swing bridge, cross the Soča and go uphill to the road. Turn R along the road briefly then go L uphill on a steep path with stone steps, which follows the line of former WW1 trenches, going through a gully with a large rock suspended above. Road works in early 2023 blocked access to this path

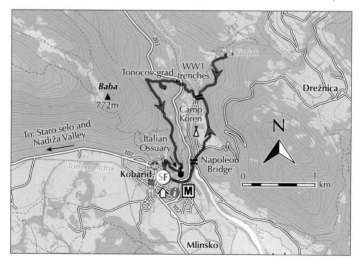

temporarily. After 30mins from the road you'll reach a junction. Turn L here to arrive at **Tonocov grad** (also called Stari grad), a site which was settled from at least the Roman period and had over 20 houses and several churches in the fifth century. Follow a path W from the junction below Tonocov grad, through forest and passing a trail on your L which goes up to Veliki Rob, a viewpoint on the slopes of Baba. Bear L, to arrive at the Italian Ossuary, 30mins from Tonocov grad.

The **Italian Ossuary** (*Italijanska kostnica*, also called the Italian Charnel House) houses the remains of over 7000 known and unknown Italian soldiers who died along this part of the Soča Front in WW1. It stands on a small hill, Gradič nad Kobaridom, surrounding the 17th-century Church of St Anthony, and was built in the shape of an octagon, with three concentric terraces diminishing in size. The ossuary was built in 1938, and is the work of Italian architect Giovanni Grappa, whose other works include the huge Military Memorial of Monte Grappa in the mountains above Treviso, and the sculptor Giannino Castiglioni. It's a grand and incredibly sobering spot, surrounded by the mountains which line the Soča Valley, stained red in the evening light.

Follow the asphalt road downhill from the Italian Ossuary, then go L down a path which leads back to the Kobarid Museum.

STAGE 13
Kobarid to Bovec

Start	Kobarid
Finish	Bovec
Distance	21km
Total ascent	445m
Total descent	230m
Time	7hrs
Terrain	Rocky paths beside the river with some stepped sections, 4x4 tracks and a short section on asphalt
Maximum altitude	464m (Bovec)
Transport	Two buses a day from Kobarid S to Tolmin
Facilities	Plenty of hotels, guesthouses and restaurants in Bovec; in Trnovo there's Apartma Matajurc, and Camp Trnovo has wooden chalets

This is a beautiful stretch of trail alongside the emerald green River Soča, with a bit more up and down than you might be expecting, and finishing in the lovely little town of Bovec. It's possible to make a short detour to get a closer look at the huge Boka waterfall.

From the centre of Kobarid, follow the road down to the **Napoleon Bridge**, cross the Soča and turn L. Pass the turnoff to **Camp Koren** then go L on a gravel road beside a lone eco toilet. Follow the broad track above the L bank of the Soča, passing the swing bridge on your L, and keep straight ahead passing the trail to the Kozjak Waterfall (see the recommended excursion from Kobarid) on your R. Descend to a side stream, cross the footbridge, and follow the path alongside the L bank of the Soča.

Along with the Soča Gorge (see the recommended side trip from Bovec), this stretch alongside the **river** between Kobarid and Trnovo is one of the most beautiful parts of the Soča. It can get quite hot in the summer (there's very little shade) so aim to get started early in the day.

Shortly before Trnovo ob Soči, 2hrs from Kobarid, cross the swing bridge to the R bank of the Soča (passing the stamp on the far side) then immediately turn R along a path (the beginning of this is not very clear initially, but if you find

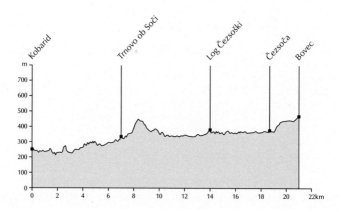

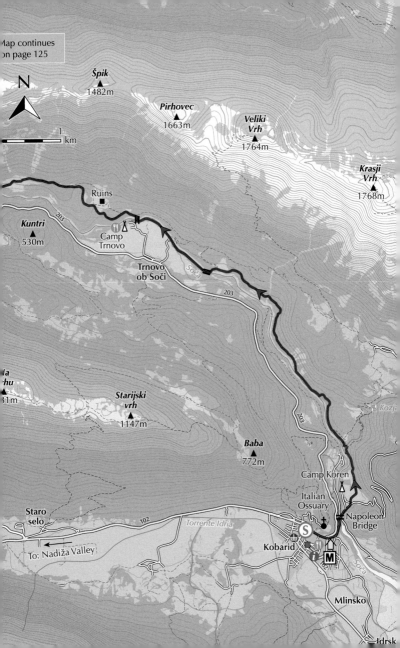

Map continues on page 125

N

1 km
km

▲ Špik
1482m

▲ Pirhovec
1663m

▲ Veliki Vrh
1764m

▲ Krasji Vrh
1768m

Ruins ■

▲ Kuntri
530m

Camp Trnovo

Trnovo ob Soči

203

Soča

203

Na hu 1m

▲ Starijski vrh
1147m

▲ Baba
772m

Camp Koren

Italian Ossuary

203

Napoleon Bridge

Soča

Kozj

Staro selo

102

Torrente Idria

Kobarid

S

i

M

To: Nadiža Valley

Mlinsko

Idrsk

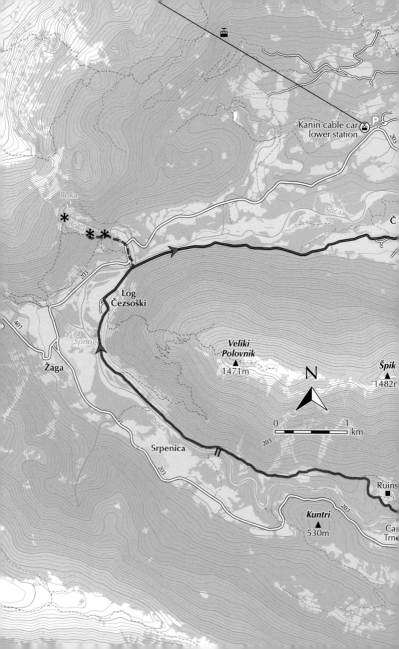

Kanin cable car
lower station

P
203

Boka

Soča

Č

Boka

*

**

203

Log
Čezsoški

Žaga

401

Uča
Spring

*Veliki
Polovnik*
1471m

Špik
1482r

N

0   1
                    km

203

Soča

Srpenica

203

Ruins

Kuntri
530m

203

Ca
Trn

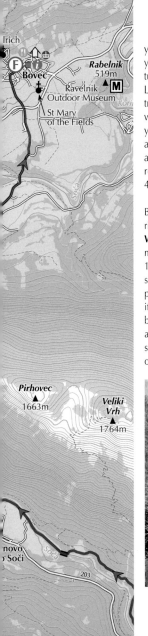

yourself walking up a 4x4 track towards Trnovo, you're missed it). When you reach **Camp Trnovo**, turn R and cross another swing bridge back to the L bank of the Soča, and turn L along a rough 4x4 track. Bear L twice more then head uphill through woodland, passing some ruins and a stone well on your R. The trail drops down a bit closer to the river again, and passes a path to another swing bridge and then a spring on your L. Go onto the asphalt road, to reach the village of **Log Čezsoški**, 1hr 45mins from Camp Trnovo.

Beyond Log Čezsoški on the opposite side of the river, a valley branches off to the N, where the **Boka Waterfall** – Slovenia's highest – shoots out of the mountainside and roars down the cliff in a single, 106m leap, with an additional 30m down steep slopes below that. It's a hugely impressive sight, in particular after rain, and well worthy of a detour if you have time (allow 45mins return). Cross the bridge after Log Čezsoški, and keep straight ahead along the road for around 200 metres to reach the start of a gravelly path on your L, above the R bank of the Boka stream. Follow this uphill, steeply in

Hunting tower on the edge of open meadows near Čezsoča

places, to a viewpoint facing the Boka waterfall across the valley. Return to the bridge and cross to the L bank of the Soča, and continue along the Juliana.

Go through the village, and past a road bridge over the Soča (or, cross the bridge if you want to make a detour to see the Boka falls). Follow the asphalt road along the L bank of the river, which is broader here and braided, with views of the Boka falls on the opposite side. Go through a large area of open pasture with some expansive views of the surrounding mountains, into the village of **Čezsoča**. Pass the church and a WW2 memorial, then bear L past the Prijon Sports Centre and cross the bridge over the Soča, following the asphalt road uphill on the other side. Bear L onto a track past the airstrip (there's a WW1 memorial a couple of minutes further along the asphalt road), go straight ahead at the roundabout, pass Hotel Alp then turn R onto Trg golobarskih žrtev, the main square in **Bovec**.

BOVEC

Bovec is a lovely little mountain town, set amid a level area on the R bank of the Soča, near its confluence with the Koritnica and below the towering slopes of Mt Kanin. Market stalls selling street food on the main square gives it a lively atmosphere in the summer months, while the view of the peaks above the Trenta Valley catching the evening light is truly sublime. The Church of St Ulrich (Cerkev sv. Urh) in the centre of town dates from the 13th century, and was rebuilt in Baroque style in the 1700s, with further changes in the 19th century. The unusual thing about the church is that, during the 18th-century remodelling, its axis was changed from the usual E–W to N–S. The Ravelnik Outdoor Museum just outside town has a restored series of trenches and bunkers from WW1.

There's plenty of scope for spending an extra day or two around Bovec – it's well worth taking the cable car up to Mt Kanin for example, from where there are rocky trails along the border ridge, and a popular via ferrata route over the face of Prestreljenik, culminating in a spectacular rock window (https://kanin.si/en). Another worthwhile excursion is Svinjak, the distinctive peak E of the town – although the last 150m or so are quite steep and exposed. The one you really shouldn't miss however is the hike to the Soča Gorge, described below. It's a full day's hiking, so you'd need an extra night in Bovec.

Accommodation in Bovec includes the lovely Sanje ob Soči (www.sanjeobsoci.com), Martinov hram (www.martinov-hram.si), Hotel Mangart (www.hotel-mangart.com/en), Bovec Holiday House (www.booking.com/hotel/si/bovec-holiday-house) and Apartma Tobi (www.booking.com/hotel/si/tobi). The Tourist Information Office is just off the main square.

Start/finish	Bovec
Distance	21km
Total ascent/descent	240m
Time	6hrs
Terrain	Good paths alongside the Soča, with a couple of short sections on 4x4 tracks and asphalt
Maximum altitude	495m

East from Bovec, the River Soča enters its most spectacular section, the Soča Gorge. There are actually two gorges, the Velika korita Soče (Great Soča Gorge) and the Mala korita Soče (Little Soča Gorge) – this excursion visits both, but it's the second, further one that you really won't want to miss. It's an easy though quite long day trip, best enjoyed between two nights in Bovec.

From the centre of Bovec, follow a road SE from opposite Letni vrt restaurant, crossing a stream and following Alpe Adria Trail signs past the little **Church of St Mary of the Fields** (Cerkev sv. Device marije v polju). Cross the main road and go straight ahead on a 4x4 road leading up over the Rabelnik hill, joining an asphalt road on the other side and following this downhill to **Camp Liža**. Go L through the camp and cross a footbridge over the Koritnica near its confluence with the Soča.

Follow a meandering path above the R bank of the Soča then crossing a foot-bridge to the L bank. Pass the **Kršovec Gorge**, before crossing back to the R bank. The trail hugs close to or goes along the road here, before crossing back to the L bank. Moving away from the river slightly, the trail follows a broad track, passing a small sculpture garden on the R, then going onto an asphalt road and crossing the Lepenjica to arrive at **Kamp Klin**. Follow the asphalt road beside the Soča to reach a parking area and the beginning of the **Little Soča Gorge**, a popular spot for swimming. Staying on the L bank, follow the road past the bridge then bear L on a path which goes through woodland, ascending slightly, then descending to the rocky terraces above the **Great Soča Gorge**.

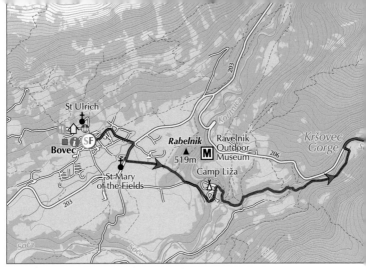

Great Soča Gorge

Around 750m long, the Great Soča Gorge reaches 15m deep and is only a couple of metres wide in places – the water twisting below smooth, overhanging limestone cliffs, with small streams and springs pouring down its sides, and its vivid turquoise pools pierced by shafts of sunlight. There's another viewpoint further up the gorge, but it's not as impressive as this one and as it's near a car park it tends to be busier.

Return to **Bovec** by the same route.

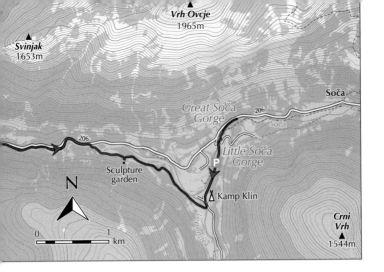

STAGE 14

Bovec to Log pod Mangartom

Start	Bovec
Finish	Log pod Mangartom
Distance	12km
Total ascent	340m
Total descent	150m
Time	4hrs
Terrain	Good forest paths and some 4x4 tracks
Maximum altitude	645m (Log pod Mangartom)
Transport	None
Facilities	A handful of guesthouses and a couple of restaurants in Log pod Mangartom

This is a beautiful walk up the Koritnica valley, taking in a small gorge as well as the fortress at Kluž, with lovely views ahead to Mangart.

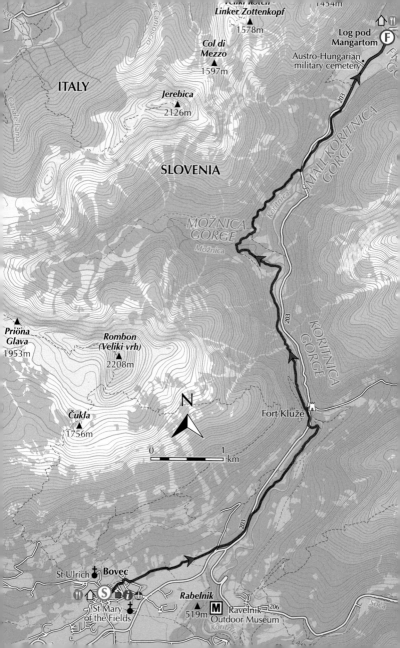

ITALY

Linker Zottenkopf
1578m

Col di
Mezzo
1597m

Jerebica
2126m

SLOVENIA

MOŽNICA
GORGE

Možnica

Prisňa
Glava
1953m

Rombon
(Veliki vrh)
2208m

Čukla
1756m

N

0   1
━━━━━━━━━━━━━━ km

1434m

Log pod
Mangartom

F

Austro-Hungarian
military cemetery

MALI KORITNICA GORGE

Koritnica

203

KORITNICA
GORGE

203

Fort Kluže

203

St Ulrich   Bovec

S

St Mary
of the Fields

Rabelnik

519m   M   Ravelnik
Outdoor Museum

1206

Soča

Koritn

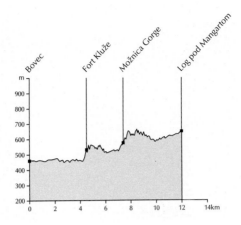

Walk NE from the main square in Bovec past Martinov Hram, Mercator and a bakery, then turn L at the bend. Go R at the water trough, cross the water channel by the footbridge, turn R and go straight ahead along an asphalt lane, becoming a path then a 4x4 track. Bear L when you exit the trees, crossing a meadow with Svinjak ahead. Cross a 4x4 track and go ahead along a track through woodland, then L onto the main road, and R downhill on a gravel track. It's a nice track through forest, passing a trail on your L (part of the Walk of Peace or Pot Miro). Bear L (not down over the bridge), going onto a path above the river. Turn L and up a series of wooden steps, then R onto the main road to arrive at the **Fort Kluže**, 1hr 20mins from Bovec.

> **Fort Kluže** (Trdnjava Kluže) stands above the Koritnica where it has carved a narrow gorge, 60m deep, below the steep slopes of Mt Rombon. The Venetians built a wooden fortress here in the 1400s, which the Habsburgs replaced with a stone one in the 16th century, effectively controlling the road to the Predil Pass. This was taken by Napoleon in 1797, and subsequently pulled down, and the Austrians then built a new fortress in the 1880s, along with Fort Hermann on the slopes above. Sheltered from Italian shelling, Kluže survived WW1 largely unscathed, although after WW2 the W rampart and portal, which originally ran across the road, were removed. There's a museum inside, and cultural events in the summer (www.kluze.net) – and there's a dizzying view down into the gorge from the bridge.

Cottage in the Koritnica Valley

Follow the path opposite the fort, which leads into a cave gallery through the base of the cliff, used in WW1. Go through the tunnel, passing a side chamber, then at the far end of the tunnel, continue along a forest path, and bear R and slightly downhill where the path forks. The path contours the forested slopes above the Koritnica, moving closer to the river with tantalising views of Mangart ahead. Go through a gate and cross a meadow, then up into forest again above the R bank of the Možnica stream. A short side trail on the R, quite steep and loose, descends slightly towards the stream, from where there's a good view of the Možnica falls. The Možnica is sometimes referred to locally as the Nemčlja. Continue along the main trail, which becomes steeper here and slightly exposed, zigzagging up with the aid of some steel cables then bearing R, to reach a footbridge over the **Možnica Gorge**, 1hr 40mins from Kluže.

The **Možnica** has carved a beautiful gorge at this point, whooshing below the bridge between tight cliffs, and the surrounding area feels much wilder than the better-known Soča. On the far side of the bridge, a path on the L ascends to a meadow, from where it's possible to continue W on a 4x4 track then a path across steep scree to the Možnica spring – but it's a fairly long detour (at least 90mins return), and the path is steep and faint in places.

Cross the footbridge and continue straight ahead along the path, then go onto a 4x4 track, passing a lone stone cottage on your R. There are beautiful views of Mangart ahead from this point – at 2679m, the third highest peak in Slovenia – framed by the steep sides of the valley. Bear R and follow the 4x4 track down towards the Koritnica, ignoring a turning on your R. The Juliana stamp for stage 14 is beside the bridge crossing the stream. At 45mins from the Možnica Gorge, cross a stream to reach a parking area, then go L onto the main road – though it's worth turning R first to see the **Small Koritnica Gorge** (Mala korita Koritnice) from the road bridge, just 50 metres away. Cross the road and turn R, following a 4x4 track parallel to the river, then rejoin the main road and follow this into **Log pod Mangartom**.

LOG POD MANGARTOM

The village of Log pod Mangartom lies on the road to the Predil Pass, at the point where the Predelica flows down into the Koritnica, and the latter bends NE below an amphitheatre of peaks over 2500m, including Mangart and Jalovec. It's a beautiful setting, but also the setting of one of the worst natural disasters in Slovenia in recent decades. In November 2000, the upper part of the village, including several houses and the bridge, was destroyed by a huge landslide, which came down during a prolonged spell of heavy rain, and claimed seven lives.

Running NW from the village below Mt Kolovrat, the Štoln Tunnel was a 4.8km drainage tunnel built in 1903 to drain water from the lead mine at Cave del Predil. Following its construction it was used by miners from Log pod Mangartom as a convenient shortcut to reach the mine, rather than going over the Predil Pass, and in WW1 Austrian troops added a narrow gauge railway in the tunnel, so that it could be used to move troops and supplies.

There was once a mosque in the village, built by Bosnian troops serving in the Austrian army in WW1, but pulled down by Italy following the war. This was to be the only mosque built in Slovenia until 2013. The Austro-Hungarian military cemetery in Log pod Mangartom is one of the best preserved in the country, and includes several *nišans* – traditional Muslim headstones, marking the graves of the Bosnian soldiers who died here.

If you have time, take a stroll further along the Koritnica Valley – turn R off the main road just after the bridge over the Predelice, for increasingly good views of the surrounding peaks – or if you cross to the L bank of the Koritnica from the village, a trail leads up the Fratarica Gorge to several attractive waterfalls, including the 50m high Parabola waterfall. One more thing – along with the Vršič pass, the Predil Pass forms a popular circuit for motorbike tours, meaning that especially during the European Bike Week held in Carinthia in early September, this otherwise peaceful spot can get quite noisy.

Accommodation in Log pod Mangartom includes Hiša Urška (www.booking.com/hotel/si/hisa-urska), Kronotop Hostel which has doubles/twins as well as small dorms (www.booking.com/hotel/si/kronotop-hostel), Joe's Place (www.booking.com/hotel/si/joe-39-s-place) and Vila Valanga (www.booking.com/hotel/si/vila-valanga).

STAGE 15

Log pod Mangartom to Tarvisio

Start	Log pod Mangartom
Finish	Tarvisio
Distance	22km
Total ascent	665m
Total descent	560m
Time	7hrs
Terrain	Good forest paths, steep in places, on the way up to the pass; a long stretch of road walking on the other side, a large part of which can be avoided by taking a local bus
Maximum altitude	1160m (Passo di Predil)
Transport	A bus runs from Cave del Predil to Tarvisio; trains from Tarvisio Boscoverde to Trieste
Facilities	Plenty of hotels, guesthouses and restaurants in Tarvisio; there's a café in Cave del Predil, and a couple of apartments

This stage climbs up to the Predil Pass, taking in some exceptionally beautiful waterfalls on the Predelica stream, before crossing the border into Italy, passing the lovely Lago del Predil and descending to Tarvisio. Unfortunately the route down the other side to Tarvisio follows an asphalt road for most of the way – I suggest you avoid some of this by taking a local bus between Cave del Predil and Plezzut. There are plans to establish a longer alternative route for the Juliana N of Cave del Predil, leading NW via the valley of the Rio del Fredo. Note that a lower set of falls on the Predelica, much closer to Log pod Mangartom, are much harder to reach, involving some difficult and exposed scrambling through an area of quite unstable rock following the landslide in 2000 – so not included here, and best avoided.

Predil (Passo di Predil) is the Italian spelling of the pass; the Slovene spelling is Predel (Prelaz Predel). Tarvisio is Trbiž in Slovene. The Predelica stream is sometimes called the Predilnica.

Follow the main road uphill through Log pod Mangartom, cross the bridge, then immediately turn L between houses, and follow a path uphill on the R. The trail climbs steadily through forest. There are glimpses of waterfalls, and some loose, narrow sections secured with cables. After 1hr from Log pod Mangartom, arrive at a junction. The path on the R leads in 15mins up to Strmec na Predelu, a village spread along the road and a much-photographed view with the soaring peaks beyond. Turn L, then 10mins later bear L again following signs to the Zaročenca Waterfall. Pass a stone wall on your R and go downhill to reach the Predelica stream, bear R then ford the river where it's shallow. This brings you to a wedge of boulders between the two arms of the Predelica on the L and the Mangarstki

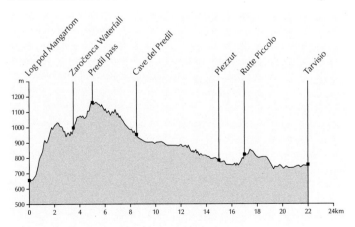

135

Map continues on page 139

Riofreddo

SS54

Muda

Cima Alpel
1743m

Monte Re
1912m

Prima
1909m

N

Quarta
1882m

0   1
km

Monte Sciober grande
1833m

Piccolo Monte Re
1500m

Canale Bosco Nero

ITALY

Canale Risonante

Mala Ruša – Punta dei Camosci
1922m

Cave del Predil (Rabelj)

M

Mont
p

Monte Guarda – Skutnik
1868m

Ursic di Raibl – Vršič
1918m

ôf del Lago
761m

SS54

Rio Lago

Veliki Grintavec
1943m

Veliki Hlebec – Grande Hlebeg
1799m

nale Malga

Planja
1553m

Cima Predil – Predelske glave
1622m

Mangartski potok

SS54

SP76

Lago del Predil

Canale Predil

Batteria Sella Predil

Fort (ruins)

203

Strmec na Predelu

Predel/Predil Pass

Zarocenca

Smaragdno oko

Predelski

ITALY

Kolovrat
1454m

SLOVENIA

Predrica

Col di Mezzo
1597m

Military cemetery

Log pod Mangartom

S

Koritnica

203

FRATARICA GORGE

Jerebica
2126m

Koritnica

Petricevec
1229m

Unamed waterfall above the confluence of the Mangarstki potok and the Predelica

potok on the R, with the impressive **Zaročenca falls** on your R, and an unnamed waterfall (possibly only visible after sufficient rain, as on my visit) on the L.

Follow a faint trail through the boulders then go steeply uphill following steps made from wooden blocks and over tree roots, with the Mangarstki potok coming down on your R. Further uphill, cross a small stream, and pass a ruined bunker on your R, with more falls visible below. Go past a path on your R leading up to Viadukt pri Mlinču, then bear L down to **Smaragdno oko** ('emerald eye'), a shallow, brightly coloured pool between rushing falls, 45mins from the Zaročenca falls.

Continue along the L bank of the Predelica, passing a side stream on your L. It's possible to ford the Predelica here, and follow the side stream for 5mins to see the 50m high **Predelski falls** (Predelski slap) – there's a marked path, but after rain (when the falls will be most impressive) the Predelica can be a bit deep to ford comfortably here.

A little further along the L bank of the Predelica, cross another side stream, and go uphill passing a small waterfall on your R. Bear R, then go R at a stone wall. Follow the edge of a field up to a cottage, and go L onto the main road, 45mins from Smaragdno oko. A couple of minutes along the road, you'll arrive at a sign marking the Slovenian/Italian border on the **Predil Pass** – so, welcome to Italy! The Juliana stamp for Stage 15 is beside the road here.

Three hundred metres beyond the border, you'll pass the remains of **Batteria Sella Predil** on your L, built by Austria in the 1890s to control the road to the pass and the valley below – its guns had a range of seven kilometres. The battery sustained little damage in WW1 (its guns were moved to a new battery), so it's still relatively intact. (The ruins of another fort lie further back along the road on the Slovenian side – this was built during the Napoleonic Wars, but by WW1 was only used for storage.) Follow the main road straight ahead, then at the third hairpin go straight ahead on a broad track, passing a trail on your L leading down to Lago del Predil.

It would be a pity to pass **Lago del Predil** without seeing it, so follow the path downhill to the car park, beside the shore of the lake. Lago del Predil lies in a glacier-scoured valley, which runs SW up to the Sella Nevea, a pass on the N slopes of Mt Kanin/Monte Canin. It is fed by the Rio Lago, which then flows out from the N end of the lake, and sits below the jagged summit of 2666m Jôf Fuart, which towers above the NW shore of the lake. There's a small island, the residue of a moraine, with the ruins of a house on it. Lago del Predil is a popular spot for swimming, and there's a small seasonal restaurant on the other side of the outlet of the Rio Lago. Austria built a fort on the opposite shore of the lake in the 1880s, which was largely destroyed in WW1. Allow 10mins each way to reach the lake from the main trail.

Continuing past the Lago del Predil path, descend towards the town passing some large falls on your R. Go L onto the main road, then R into the centre of **Cave del Predil**, passing the Church of St Anna on your L and the small Mining Museum (Museo Minario), to reach a bus stop on your L, a little under 1hr from the border (not including time at the lake).

Cave del Predil ('Rabelj' in Slovenian) is a small lead and zinc mining town, first mentioned in the 14th century when the area belonged to the Prince-Bishopric of Bamberg. The town and surrounding area were never taken by Venice, and it was sold to the Habsburgs in the 1750s. Over the centuries, more than 150km of galleries were excavated, on 25 levels. The mines were worked until 1991; following their closure, the population went into decline. There's an interesting Mining Museum in the town (Museo della Tradizione Mineraria, www.museitarvisio.it/museo3).

The route from Cave del Predil follows the main road or tracks alongside it for the next six kilometres or so – the surrounding scenery is lovely enough,

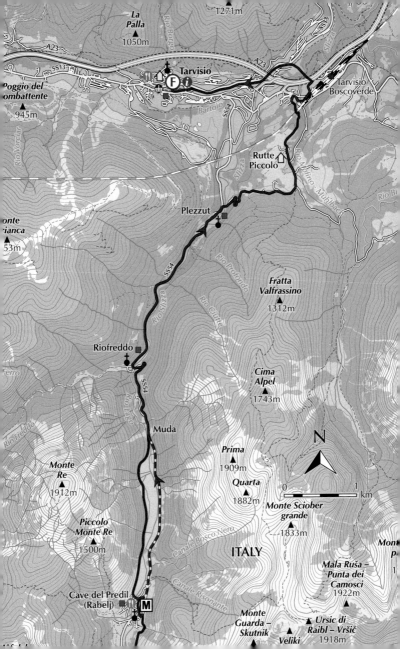

but the walking not so rewarding, so I suggest taking the bus from Cave del Predil to Plezzut, at which point the trail branches off the main road (still on asphalt for part of the way, but more enjoyable). It's the #204 bus you want – there are several services a day, but a big gap in the timetable between 13:45 and 18:30, so you should really aim to get the one at 13:45. For time-tables go to https://tplfvg.it/it/il-viaggio/costruisci-il-tuo-orario, scroll down to Cerca gli Orari and type in Cave del Predil.

If you prefer to walk from Cave del Predil, you can either stay on the L bank of the Rio Lago, following a 4x4 track before crossing back to the R bank at Muda, or continue on the main road. Both these routes converge at Muda, from where you should continue along the main road past **Riofreddo**, at the confluence of the Rio Freddo and Rio Lago (after which they become the Rio Slizza), and on to **Plezzut**.

From the bus stop opposite the small church in Plezzut, continue along the main road very briefly then turn R onto a minor asphalt road, crossing a bridge over the Rio Slizza and heading uphill. Go straight ahead through the village of **Rutte Piccolo** (there's an Albergo Diffuso on the L), then bear R on a farm track. Go across a field and under the pylons, heading downhill with Tarvisio ahead. The path is unclear here – it should go straight ahead just above where the **railway line** emerges from a tunnel, then L to reach the busy main road where that goes

River Slizza near Plezzut

into a tunnel on your R (if you miss the path, follow the more obvious asphalt lane downhill from the L side of the field, then go R along the main road to rejoin the 'correct' route just before the tunnel). Follow an asphalt lane parallel to the railway tracks, then turn L onto a cycle path (part of the Alpe Adria Cycle Trail). Cross the viaduct high over the Rio Slizza, then bear L along the asphalt cycle path, passing the medieval tower on the SE corner of the old town, before turning R into the main square (Piazza Unità) in the centre of **Tarvisio**.

TARVISIO

Tarvisio (Trbiž in Slovene) lies in the Val Canale, an important trade route since Roman times which ran towards Aquileia and the Adriatic in one direction, and up into Carinthia (at that time the province of Noricum) in the other. From the early 11th century, along with the rest of the Val Canale down as far as Pontebba, it was owned by the Prince-Bishopric of Bamberg, an ecclesiastical state within the Holy Roman Empire. Another reason for the area's importance was its highly prized mining industry, including iron, lead and zinc. It was sold to the Habsburgs in the 18th century, and didn't become part of Italy until the end of WW1 – until which time the main languages spoken in the area were German and Slovene (you'll find an inscription in German on the main portal of Tarvisio's 15th-century parish church).

On Piazza Unità, you'll find the Parish Church of Sts Peter and Paul (Chiesa dei Santi Pietro e Paolo), built in the 15th century on the remains of an earlier church. The inscription above the portal (in German) gives the date of its completion as 1445. On the N side of the church is the Torre Nord, one of the remaining medieval towers. Tarvisio Forest, to the N of the town, is Italy's largest state forest.

Accommodation in Tarvisio includes Hotel Edelhof (www.hoteledelhof. it/en), Hotel Haberl (www.hotelhaberl.com/en), Fiocco di Neve (www.book ing.com/hotel/it/fiocco-di-neve-tarvisio12) and Hotel Raibl (www.hotelraibl. com/en). The Tourist Information Office is on Via Roma. The railway station (Tarvisio Boscoverde) is on the E side of town, near the start of Stage 16.

STAGE 16

Tarvisio to Kranjska Gora

Start	Tarvisio
Finish	Kranjska Gora
Distance	19.5km
Total ascent	180m
Total descent	130m
Time	5hrs
Terrain	Easy walking mainly along a cycle track, formerly a narrow gauge railway
Maximum altitude	870m (Rateče)
Transport	Buses and trains from Tarvisio; buses from Rateče to Kranjska Gora
Facilities	Plenty of hotels, restaurants and guesthouses in Kranjska Gora; a few restaurants and guesthouses in Rateče and Podkoren

The final stage of the main Juliana circuit takes you back over the border into Slovenia, passing some lovely views up to the knot of jagged summits on the N flanks of Mangart on the way, and the utterly breathtaking Zeleci Nature Reserve.

The Juliana follows a rather strange choice of route out of Tarvisio, choosing to turn off the cycle path onto main roads rather than retracing your steps further along the cycle path as on the previous stage. My advice is to ignore the official route and retrace your steps from Stage 15 as far as the railway line.

From Piazza Unità, return to the cycle path and follow this E. If you want to follow the official route (my suggestion is that you don't, and continue straight ahead along the cycle path instead), turn off the cycle path down a flight of steps and onto the road at a hairpin, then cross the Rio Slizza with the stadium on your L. Go L along the main road then bear L along a minor asphalt road to rejoin the route from Stage 15 just NE of the main road entering a tunnel. Turn L parallel to the railway lines, passing the cycle route on your L (if you simply retrace your steps from Stage 15 as suggested, you'll arrive at this point).

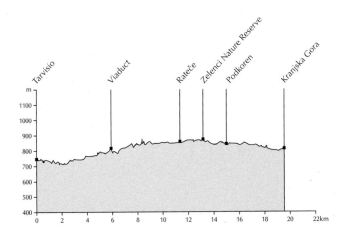

Keep following the asphalt lane beside the railway lines, passing the station, **Tarvisio Boscoverde**. Bear R under the railway line, then bear L, keeping to the cycle path, with a view of the viaduct over the Rio Bianco on your L. Go straight ahead across a road, with some amazing views on your R around 30mins beyond this as you cross a long viaduct over the headwaters of the Rio Bianco, which twist up a wild valley towards the jagged outline of the Breitkofel, Torre Val Romana and Picco di Mezzodi, which lie on the N side of Mangart, soon followed by another bridge over the Rio Nero.

'Traffic' on the Juliana Trail, where it follows the course of the former Tarvisio-Ljubljana Railway, near Rateče

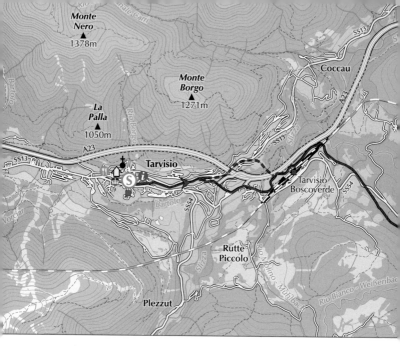

The cycle path you are following here, with its bridges and viaducts, was part of a former railway line. This was the **Tarvisio–Ljubljana Railway**, a single track line built by Austria following the construction of the Rudolfsbahn (named after Crown Prince Rudolf, and linking St Valentin near Linz with Tarvisio). The line opened in 1870, however traffic decreased following the closure of the Italian/Slovenian border here after WW2, with the section between Tarvisio and Jesenice closing in the late 1960s. E of Kranjska Gora the cycle route is known as the D2, some of which you've already followed on Stage 1.

Pass a trail on your R (where the Alpe Adria Trail comes down from the beautiful Laghi di Fusine), then cross the border back into Slovenia, 1hr 45mins from Tarvisio Boscoverde station. Turn L down a track to reach the main road. The Juliana stamp for Stage 16 is beside the road here. Pass a bus stop and Gostilna Ponca on your R, then bear L along an asphalt lane behind the petrol station into **Rateče**. The peak due N of Rateče is Peč/Ofen/Monte Forno, which marks the tri-partite border of Slovenia, Austria and Italy. Pass Gostilna Šurc and Vila Moj Mir, and some beautifully renovated façades. At the far end of town keep straight

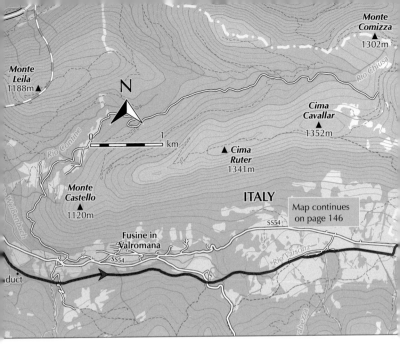

ahead (not L as shown on some early gpx routes), then go L onto the main road, to arrive at a car park and the entrance to **Zelenci Nature Reserve** on your R, 40mins after crossing the border.

Zelenci Nature Reserve is just a 5min detour off the Juliana, and should most definitely be considered an integral part of the route. Follow the path through the trees, bearing L to reach the edge of a small lake, with wooden board-walks and a wooden viewing tower. It's an exquisitely beautiful place, and the water is an almost unbelievably intense colour, with shades of green and turquoise, surrounded by extensive reed beds. It was formed following the retreat of the huge Planica glacier in the last Ice Age, which left a much larger lake trapped behind a moraine wall. A river eventually cut through this and drained the lake, leaving the small wetland area around Zelenci. The small lake is the source of the Sava Dolinka, with water welling up from the porous chalk lakebed in tiny jets (these are actually the re-emergence of another stream, the Nadiža, which springs from a rock face in the Tamar Valley but soon disappears underground).

145

Zelenci Nature Reserve

Continue along the main road then turn R onto a gravel path, which soon bears R over a wooden footbridge, crossing the water channels and reed beds of the Blata marsh, downstream from the Sava Dolinka source. Turn L along the

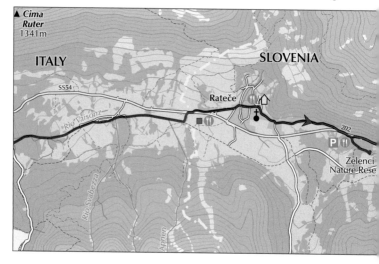

cycle path, then L and across the main road into **Podkoren**. Go under the road and turn R, then bear L, passing a shrine on your L and going straight ahead over a footbridge, onto a farm track. Follow the edge of the field, then take a gravel path on your L through forest, and go R onto a 4x4 track. Continue beside the L bank of the Sava Dolinka, passing sports fields, then turn R over the bridge and straight ahead on a gravel road. Turn L onto a path then R onto the asphalt road. Turn L and stride down Kolodvorska ulica, to arrive at the tourist information office in **Kranjska Gora**, just over 2hrs beyond Zelenci Nature Reserve – and a 270-kilometre circuit of the Julian Alps since you started.

KRANJSKA GORA

Kranjska Gora sits at the mouth of the Pišnica Valley, which runs S from the Upper Sava Valley towards Razor, Triglav and other giants, with a road climbing W from the valley to the Vršič Pass, before dropping down to the Trenta and Soča valleys. The undisputed outdoor sports capital of Slovenia, it lies near the edge of Triglav National Park and at the heart of a whole host of hiking trails, both in the Julian Alps and the Karawanke, and hosts the slalom and giant slalom events of the FIS Alpine Ski World Cup. Tourism gradually arrived from the late 19th century, with the opening of the Tarvisio–Ljubljana

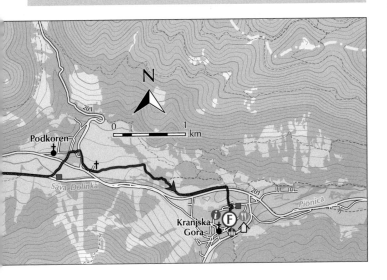

railway line, and it was on Vitranc, just W of the town, that Slovenia's oldest ski resort was opened, in 1948.

The Church of the Assumption of the Virgin Mary (Cerkev Device Marije Vnebovzete) dates from the 15th century, and has some beautiful rib vaulting. A walk down the Pišnica Valley to Lake Jasna makes for a good short excursion, or further than this up towards the Vršič Pass you'll find the Russian Chapel, which stands as a memorial to several hundred Russian prisoners of war, swept to their death by an avalanche in early 1916 while building the military road over the pass. Also it's only a 2hr hike from nearby Rateče up to the tripartite border peak, Peč.

Accommodation includes Gostilna pri Martinu (www.booking.com/hotel/si/julijana-turizem), Ramada Hotel and Suites (www.wyndhamhotels.com/en-uk/ramada), Apartments Juliana (www.booking.com/hotel/si/apartments-pri-martinu), Boutique Hotel Skipass (https://www.skipasshotel.si/en) and Apartment la Terraza (www.booking.com/hotel/si/apartment-la-terraza). Given that you've just completed the Juliana Trail, a celebration is probably in order. For a superb meal to end your trip on, head for the excellent Mama Marija (www.skipasshotel.si/en/restaurant). The Tourist Information Office is on Kolodvorska ulica; buses stop beside the Skipass Hotel.

BRDA
EXTENSION

The village of Šmartno (Stage 19)

STAGE 17
Tolmin to Planinski dom pod Ježo

Start	Tolmin
Finish	Planinski dom pod Ježo
Distance	13km
Total ascent	1000m
Total descent	450m
Time	5hrs
Terrain	Good forest trails, some gravel roads, some asphalt walking above Volče
Maximum altitude	1114m (Na Gradu, Kolovrat)
Transport	Buses to Tolmin from Most na Soči and beyond
Facilities	A few places to eat in Volče; Rifugio Casoni Solarie is a 15min detour off the Juliana beyond Kolovrat; mountain lodge Planinski dom pod Ježo (serves food)

The Brda section of the Juliana Trail begins with a long, steady climb up to Kolovrat, an open air museum of restored trenches and bunkers from WW1, then follows the ridge above the Italian border to the mountain lodge beyond Ježa. See the section on route planning in the introduction for more information about incorporating the four-stage Brda section into the main Juliana circuit.

From the Tourist Information Office in Tolmin, walk W down the main road retracing your steps from the end of Stage 11, passing a bakery on your L, going straight ahead at the roundabout and passing a café on your R. Bear L through a pair of sculpted pillars towards the cemetery and **Church of St Ulrich** (Cerkev sv. Urh), then turn R along a path around the edge of the cemetery, and R on a path down into woodland. Pass a playground and a small wooden café/bar on your L, cross the bridge (Volčanski most) over the Soča, and turn L along an asphalt lane on the R bank. Bear R, going uphill past the **Church of St Daniel** (Cerkev sv. Danijela v Volčah) – the church dates from the 16th century but was largely destroyed in WW1 and rebuilt, and the 16th-century frescoes by Jernej of Loka (he of the fresco cycle at St Peter's Church above Begunje on Stage 3) were lost. Go L onto

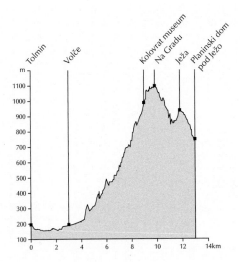

the main road into the village of **Volče**, turn R past Mercator, with the Church of St Leonard (sv. Lenart) above you on your L, then go L onto the main road, cross the bridge over the Kamnica stream, and follow the road uphill.

This stretch of asphalt walking is far from unpleasant, the road hugging the Kamnica stream, passing waterfalls and pools. After 30mins from Volče, at the first big hairpin, leave the road behind and go straight ahead up a path. Ascend through woodland, cross the stream on a wooden footbridge and continue on the R bank. Some 20 mins after leaving the road, go L on a 4x4 road, becoming a rough forest track. This contours the hillside, getting steeper, with a switchback R then L.

Pass a spring on your R and go straight across the asphalt road, then bear L up a path, and cross a track, with the valley of the Soča visible below on your R. A few final zigzags brings you up to the asphalt road. Turn L onto this to arrive at the **Kolovrat Outdoor Museum** on your R, 3hrs 15mins from the centre of Tolmin.

The **Kolovrat Outdoor Museum** (www.thewalkofpeace.com/locations/ww1-outdoor-museum-kolovrat-a-view-over-the-front) is a restored system of trenches, galleries, bunkers and gun emplacements, built by Italian troops at the beginning of WW1 along the highest part of the Kolovrat ridge. The border between Italy and Austria ran along the Kolovrat ridge, and the extensive

WW1 trench at Kolovrat

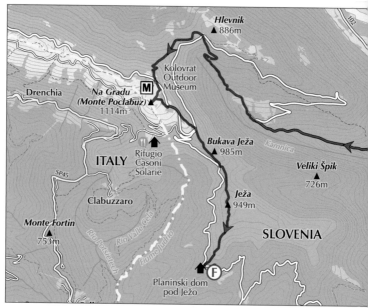

system of defence lines here allowed Italian forces to shell the Austrian positions and supply lines below, in the Soča Valley. The Kolovrat ridge was finally taken by the German Alpine Corps in October 1917, during the 12th Battle of the Isonzo – an offensive in which a young Erwin Rommel took part, and for which he was awarded the *Pour le Mérite* (the so-called 'Blue Max'). It's an extremely atmospheric place, both sad and haunting, but the setting is beautiful, and it's well worth spending half an hour or so wandering through the labyrinth of trenches as you head up towards Na Gradu.

Head uphill through the Kolovrat Outdoor Museum, following trail markings for the Juliana and the Alpe Adria Trail. The Juliana turns L just below **Na Gradu** (Monte Poclapuz, 1114m), but first it's worth continuing for 100 metres or so up to the peak, for enhanced views and a look at the summit register. The first Juliana stamp for Stage 17 is here on Na Gradu.

Follow the Juliana markings (signposted Planinski dom pod Ježo) down a rocky gully. Go R on the asphalt road briefly then L onto a path. Head uphill on a narrow forest path, then descend steeply to cross the road again at a hairpin,

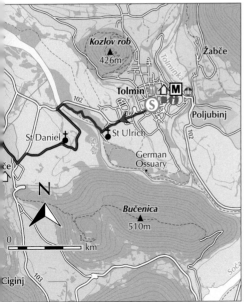

and turn L onto a broad track. Bear R on a path, descending and passing a cave on your L, and an area of trail erosion where steel cables are in place. On meeting the asphalt road again, turn L immediately on a 4x4 track, then bear R on a 4x4 track up through the trees, to reach a clearing at the top of **Ježa** (949m), 1hr 15mins from Na Gradu, with a lone bench from which to admire the lovely views E across the Soča valley. The second Juliana stamp for Stage 17 is here on Ježa.

Descend on a steep forest path, a bit unclear

View from the trail south of Ježa

in places, to reach the asphalt road opposite **Planinski dom pod Ježo**, less than 20mins from Ježa.

PLANINSKI DOM POD JEŽO

Planinski dom pod Ježo (www.pzs.si/koce.php?pid=347) stands on a hillside overlooking the valley of the River Idrija (Judrio), which marks the border with Italy. A former border guardhouse, it sleeps 34 in 4-, 12- and 18-bed dorms, and serves meals. There is no other accommodation or facilities here, and it would be a further 8km to Kambreško.

STAGE 18
Planinski dom pod Ježo to Korada

Start	Planinski dom pod Ježo
Finish	Korada
Distance	20.5km
Total ascent	720m
Total descent	670m
Time	7hrs
Terrain	A mixture of paths and 4x4 tracks with some sections on asphalt
Maximum altitude	812m (Korada)
Transport	None
Facilities	Apartma Humarji just 100 metres off the trail, 30mins beyond Kambreško www.airbnb.co.uk/rooms/35723682; mountain hut just below Korada. There's one small shop in Kambreško.

This stage continues to follow the ridge between the valleys of the Soča and the Idrija, taking in more remnants of WW1 and the striking Marijino Celje pilgrimage church above Lig, with some lovely views along the way.

Follow the asphalt road E (downhill) from Planinski dom pod Ježo, turning L at the road junction at **Vogrinki** and R onto a 4x4 road which contours the E side of a low wooded hill (Ostri Kras). Rejoin the asphalt road and follow this L past **Pušno** to reach the village of **Srednje**, around 1hr 20mins from Planinski dom pod Ježo. It's worth walking up through the village to see the small Church of Sv. Trojice, built in the 19th century and apparently financed by Emperor Franz Josef himself.

Keep following the asphalt road as it bends L past Srednje, then bear L and uphill where the road forks at the end of the village, and turn R at the hairpin onto a forest path. This ascends gradually along a ridge, to reach a clearing with good views on your L, then a trail junction where you turn L to reach the top of **Globočak**.

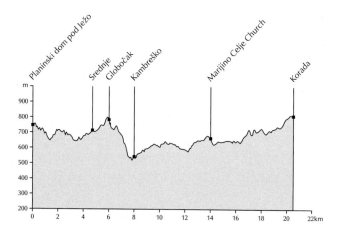

Globočak (809m) is another of the hills along the Kolovrat ridge which was well fortified by Italian troops during WW1, since it commanded good views over the Soča valley. Along with the concrete bunker and memorial on the summit, there are trenches, a cave and a water reservoir nearby.

From the trail junction descend steeply SW, then turn R onto a path downhill. This becomes a broad track, leading down across terraces to the village of **Kambreško**, 1hr 15mins from Srednje. Head down through the village, and go L onto the main road by a Partisan memorial. Bear L at the junction then go immediately R along an asphalt lane towards the Veterinary centre, with views opening out on the L. Pass a spring on the R, and pass a turning on your L to Apartma Humarji, keeping straight ahead on a 4x4 track. Go R when you reach the road, following the asphalt lane rather than the track across the fields above it. Bear R onto a broader asphalt road then go L up a 4x4 track. Pass a lone farm building on your L, and cross open pasture as the twin spires of Marijino Celje come into view. Ascend passing a shrine on your L to reach the pilgrimage Church of **Marijino Celje**, which sits atop a raised terrace above the village of Lig, 90mins from Kambreško.

There was a church on the **terrace** in the early 1300s, which was rebuilt in the 16th century. This was remodelled in the 1700s, including the addition

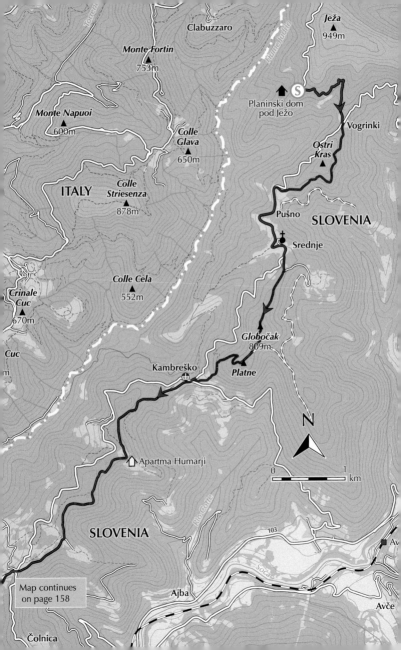

Ježa
949m

Clabuzzaro

Hrastovlje

Monte Fortin
753m

Planinski dom
pod Ježo

S

Vogrinki

Monte Napuoi
600m

*Colle
Glava*
650m

*Ostri
Kras*

Pušno

SLOVENIA

ITALY

*Colle
Striesenza*
878m

Srednje

Colle Cela
552m

*Crinale
Cuc*
670m

Globočak
809m

*Cuc
m*

Kambreško

Platne

N

Apartma Humarji

0   1
km

SLOVENIA

103

Soča

Av

Map continues
on page 158

Ajba

Avče

Čolnica

The pilgrimage Church of Marijino Celje

of the twin bell towers with pewter roofs (one of these was demolished in the 19th century, and both rebuilt in the late 1990s). It gained its importance as a pilgrimage church in 1761, following the arrival of a copy of the much-venerated wooden statue of the Virgin Mary in the Mariazell Basilica in Austria. The altar dates from 1686, and is probably by the local Pacassi workshop in Goriška Brda – it was originally installed at the important pilgrimage Church of Sveta Gora which lies fur ther down the Soča Valley (there are fantastic views of Sveta Gora on Stage 20), and was transferred to the Church of Marijino Celje 100 years later in 1786.

There are lovely views from the front terrace, especially to the N where you should be able to make out Mt Krn (and Triglav in the far distance beyond it if you're lucky), and to the S beyond Nova Gorica you can see the Adriatic on a clear day. The Juliana stamp for Stage 18 is beside a small replica of Aljažev stup, the small shelter on the summit of Triglav, just below the terrace.

Follow the asphalt lane flanked by yellow conifers, pass a shrine on your L and go straight ahead on an asphalt road. Go straight ahead at the junction then bear L (un-signposted) where the road forks. Pass a footpath on your L (leading to Kanal in under 2hrs), then immediately after a trail on the L to the **Church of St Jacob** (Cerkev sv. Jakov), take a path on your L which climbs through forest above the road. At the crest of the hill, pass another trail on your L to the church. Head downhill, crossing a track before ascending again to a clearing, from where there are some particularly good views. The church to the WNW is the pilgrimage sanctuary at Castelmonte. Ten minutes beyond the clearing go L onto an asphalt road, which leads up over open slopes with more lovely views to the NW from above the hairpin – the peak is Monte San Nicolò. Pass a road on the L to Vrtače, then where the road forks at a Partisan memorial go straight ahead on a path. Cross grassy tops then go L on a gravel road, and L on a path up through woodland, which leads you to the small **Church of St Gertrude** (Sv. Genderca) 90mins from Marijino Celje. The church was demolished during WW1, and later rebuilt. There are some benches from which to take in the views across the Soča.

It's another 10mins from the church to the top of **Korada** (811m) itself – another important defensive position of the Italians during WW1 since it marks the highest point along this part of the ridge – and another 5mins down to the small mountain hut, **Planinsko zavetišče na Koradi**.

PLANINSKO ZAVETIŠČE NA KORADI

Planinsko zavetišče na Koradi (www.pdbrda.si/index.php/nasa-planinska-koca) sits in a clearing among the trees, with an 11-bed dorm, and evening meals. It was built in the 1980s, above the site of a former bunker, cave and gun emplacement used by Italian troops during WW1. There are no shops or other facilities in the area – so just enjoy the sunset views from nearby Korada.

View north from the trail near Korada

STAGE 19
Korada to Šmartno

Start	Korada
Finish	Šmartno
Distance	11.5km
Total ascent	60m
Total descent	620m
Time	2hrs 45mins
Terrain	Easy walking on paths, 4x4 tracks and some asphalt
Maximum altitude	803m (Planinsko zavetišče na Koradi)
Transport	None until Šmartno
Facilities	Hotels, guesthouses and restaurants in Šmartno

A short, easy stage which finishes in the beautiful little town of Šmartno, at the heart of the Brda wine region.

From the hut, head SE down a forest path, bearing L where the path forks rather than entering the clearing. Go L at the asphalt road, taking a shortcut at the hairpin. Go straight ahead on an asphalt road, passing a Walk of Peace information board on your L. Turn R onto a path (no trail markings) down into a clearing, then L along a broad track, and bear R where the trail forks just below the road. Pass a tunnel on your L, walking on a gravel road briefly before regaining the asphalt road and turning R along this. Go L onto a 4x4 track before a house, and bear R along a track through livestock pastures, keeping level and bearing R. Go through a gate into woodland, straight ahead then bear L down through a clearing. Go straight across an asphalt road, then downhill on a forest path. Turn R onto an asphalt road, then immediately R onto a path very briefly, and L onto an asphalt road again. Go R at the next road junction, then L onto a 4x4 track. Bear R, then go L onto the asphalt road again, passing an apiary on your L. Keep straight ahead at the next junction, then turn R onto a path which leads up onto a small hill, where you'll find the late Baroque pilgrimage **Church of the Virgin Mary** (Cerkev Device Marije) with its crenellated tower standing above **Vrhovlje pri Kojskem**, 70mins from Planinsko zavetišče na Koradi. The Juliana stamp for Stage 19 is beside the church.

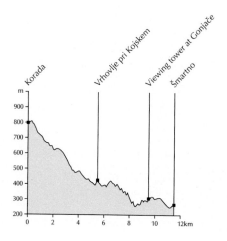

Follow the asphalt road downhill from in front of the church, through Vrhovlje pri Kojskem, with beautiful views across Goriška Brda to the SW. Go L at a junction, then R onto the main road at the bus stop. Turn L at the crossroads, passing houses then bearing R to enter pastures and then woodland on a 4x4

Crossing farmland below Korada

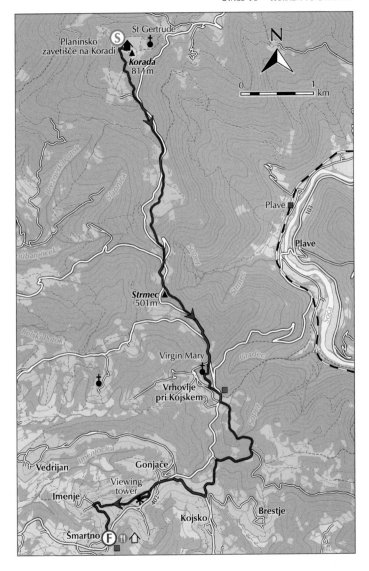

track. Turn R onto a path, then R again onto an asphalt road, passing the History of the Slovenians Memorial, formed of a series of anti-tank blocks from the 1991 Slovenian War of Independence.

Turn L down a gravel road becoming an asphalt lane, with terraces on the L and views of the rolling wine country ahead. The prominent 'castle' atop a hill to the S is actually the Church of the Holy Cross in Kojsko, which you can make a short detour to in Stage 20. Turn R onto the main road towards Šmartno, then R up an asphalt lane to reach the **viewing tower** at Gonjače, 75mins from Vrhovlje pri Kojskem.

The 23m high **viewing tower** stands on top of Mejnik, a low hill above the village of Gonjače. You can climb to the top of the three-storey tower by way of a spiral staircase, and the views from the top are stunning – from the beautiful town of Šmartno nearby, to the Dolomites, the Julian Alps and the plains of Friuli. It really catches the wind, so at the risk of stating the obvious, hold onto the railing as you're climbing the stairs if it's gusty. There's a bronze WW2 monument beside the tower, the work of Slovenian sculptor, Janez Boljka.

Retrace your steps down the asphalt lane a short way then turn L along a gravel road. Bear L at the junction, through the houses of Imenje, to arrive beside the walled old town of **Šmartno**.

Street in the small town of Šmartno

ŠMARTNO

Šmartno is one of the prettiest towns on the Juliana – small (some would call it a village), with a beautifully preserved historic core, its narrow stone-paved streets and alleys surrounded by stout medieval walls. The hill on which it stands has been a strategic position since at least Roman times, and its walls and the tall, crenellated tower of St Martin's church (patron saint of wine growers) are visible from far away across the plains. The defensive walls and towers probably date from the early 1500s, when the town was owned by the Counts of Gorica, and Šmartno was one of several fortified towns forming a defensive line against Venice (which, locals will be proud to tell you, never captured it). Five towers remain, of an original seven. Accommodation includes the excellent Hotel San Martin (www.sanmartin.si/en), which has a very good restaurant and makes its own wine, as well as Hiša Marica (www.marica.si), Aldila (www.apartmentsaldila.com/en) and Apartmaji Kumar (www.booking.com/hotel/si/apartmaji-kumar). Gostišče Turn is a cosy little place to eat in the old town, mainly serving grilled meat. The bus stop is opposite Hotel San Martin.

You're now in the Brda wine region – which although quite small is one of the best wine regions in Slovenia (and has garnered more medals per hectare than any other wine producing area in Slovenia), just over the border from the Collio wine region in Italy. The main grape variety grown here is Rebula.

STAGE 20

Šmartno to Solkan

Start	Šmartno
Finish	Solkan
Distance	15km
Total ascent	460m
Total descent	610m
Time	4hrs 30mins
Terrain	4x4 tracks and some asphalt followed by a fabulous, extended cliff path
Maximum altitude	609m (Sabatin)
Transport	Trains from Solkan to Tolmin and Jesenice in one direction, and Nova Gorica in the other
Facilities	Hotels, guesthouses and restaurants in Solkan and neighbouring Nova Gorica

The last stage of the Juliana (at least numerically) is also one of its finest, culminating in an extended romp along a cliff-top path, twisting and rocky and often buffeted by the wind, with unforgettable views across the Soča valley to the high peaks of the Julian Alps in one direction and the monastery at Sveta Gora in the other, and from its final highpoint on Mt Sabatin, an extraordinary panorama of the plains of Friuli, with the Dolomites rising like a mirage beyond. It's also the only stage on the route which I found took longer than the officially stated walking time – and I was going quite fast. A truly wonderful day out, and a fittingly grand finale to the Juliana Trail.

Retrace your route from Šmartno back through Imenje and past the viewing tower to rejoin the main road. Turn R at the junction (before reaching the roundabout) down an asphalt lane, then bear L onto a 4x4 track leading down through terraces. Don't take the promising track on your L (the signposting is a bit unclear here), but stick to the main 4x4 track, descending then heading across the terraces and bearing L, up to the main road. Turn R onto the main road into **Kojsko**, where the Juliana turns L (signposted Vinska cesta). However before leaving Kojsko, it's well worth making a short detour to visit the **Church of the Holy Cross** (Cerkev

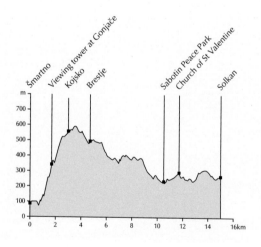

sv. Križa) – that's the picture perfect church sitting on a hill that you've caught glimpses of over the past couple of stages.

> To visit the **church** (15mins each way from Kojsko), follow the main road a bit further, past the Post Office, then bear L up an asphalt lane which becomes a 4x4 track. Bear R where the road forks, then turn R onto a path which leads up along the edge of a patch of woodland to the front of the church. The Church of the Holy Cross dates from around 1500, and contains one of the earliest Gothic altars in Slovenia. The setting is extremely beautiful, with views out across the surrounding vineyards. Return to Kojsko the same way.

The Juliana heads NE from Kojsko down an asphalt road, passing a road on your R before heading uphill through the village of Figovica, to arrive in the village of **Brestje**. Bear L and head uphill through the village, then take a R fork and go uphill on a steep concrete and gravel track. Go straight ahead over the asphalt road, up a track, bearing R near the top, and turn R onto a 4x4 road. Follow the 4x4 road along the crest of the ridge, passing a partisan memorial on your R, then going onto a forest path along the L (E) side of the ridge.

So begins one of the finest sections of the Juliana. Go L down some wooden steps, following a path with the Soča visible through the trees down below. Take a L fork, going over a bluff, and following a rocky cliff-top path with stunning views. Looking back up the Soča Valley you can make out a distant Triglav, and E across

Border markers on Mt Sabotin, looking N towards the high peaks of the Julian Alps

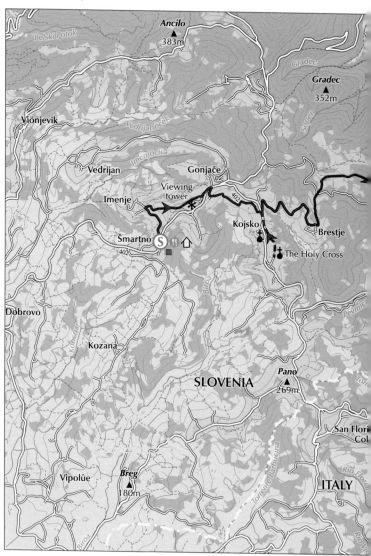

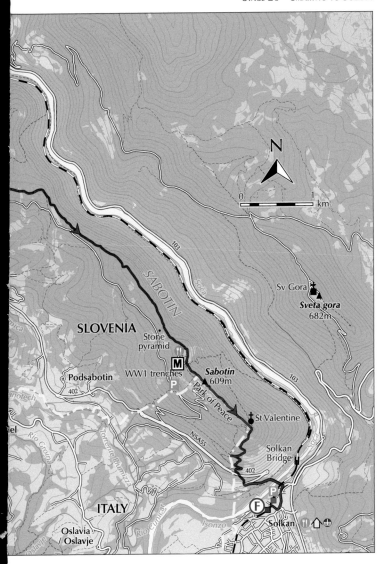

N

0   1 km

103

SABOTIN

Soča

Sv Gora ✝
Sveta gora
682m

SLOVENIA

Stone
pyramid

M

Sabotin
609m

WW1 trenches

P

Podsabotin

402

Park of Peace

103

✝ St Valentine

NSA55

Solkan
Bridge

402

ITALY

P

F

Solkan 🍴 ⌂ ♿

Oslavia
/ Oslavje

Isonzo

Rio Cunial

the valley you can see Sveta Gora with its Franciscan monastery and basilica church. Pass the remains of a pillbox on your L, and a lone bench which makes a perfect spot to stop for a well-earned breather. Pass a trail on your R, to arrive at a cross, 2hrs 15mins from Brestje. Ten minutes beyond this cross, you'll pass a **stone pyramid** on your R – one of seven built during the 1920s to mark the course of the front line during the Sixth Battle of the Isonzo in WW1.

The southern part of the **Sabotin ridge** was fortified and held by Austro-Hungarian forces at the start of WW1, until it was captured by Italy during the Sixth Battle of the Isonzo in August 1916. An extensive system of caves, gun positions (created by the Austrians on the E side of the ridge, then opened on the W side by the Italians, who were then able to shell Austrian positions on Sveta Gora) and trenches remains in place, and the area has been declared a Park of Peace, with an excellent new museum and interpretation centre in the former JNA (Yugoslav People's Army) guardhouse. There's also a small café.

Cross a system of WW1 trenches, then bear R on a broad track, walking through the car park and passing the **Park of Peace** museum. It's well worth visiting the museum, and the system of caves and tunnels on the L, which opens out below cliffs on the E side of the ridge – you'll exit the caves via the trenches on the W side of the ridge. Continuing beyond the tunnels, follow a rocky path uphill, then continue along the crest of the ridge, with absolutely stupendous views on

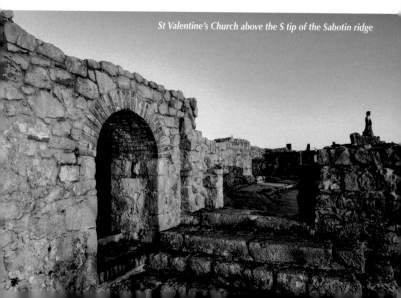

St Valentine's Church above the S tip of the Sabotin ridge

both sides, passing small border markers beside the trail and crossing the high points of Mt Sabotin (609m) and St Valentin (545m). On the latter stand the ruins of **St Valentine's Church**, which was destroyed during heavy fighting during the Isonzo battles of WW1.

Beyond St Valentine's Church, the path begins heading downhill, steeply in places, with Solkan and Nova Gorica laid out below. There are several paths branching off on your R – ignore these. Cross the main road and continue down the path, then turn L onto the main road at a hairpin, and follow it downhill to the bridge. Cross the Soča – the railway bridge on your L is the famous Solkan Bridge, more on which below. Cross the railway line, and turn R along the road into **Solkan**, passing the car park before turning R to reach the railway station, which marks the end of the route.

SOLKAN

Solkan, which grew as a village next to the town of Gorizia, was largely destroyed during the fierce fighting on the Isonzo Front in WW1. After the war it became part of the Kingdom of Italy, then following WW2 it became part of the former Yugoslavia, while Gorizia remained part of Italy. The construction of Nova Gorica (literally 'New Gorizia') next to Solkan began in the late 1940s.

Solkan lies on the railway line from Jesenice to Nova Gorica, laid down between 1900 and 1906 as part of the Neue Alpenbahnen which linked Austria with the then Habsburg-controlled port of Trieste. Just before reaching Solkan, the line crosses the Soča on the Solkan Bridge – a genuine marvel of early 20th-century engineering, and a reason in itself to take the train back towards Most na Soči. With its main arch spanning a distance of 85 metres, the Solkan bridge has the distinction of being the world's longest stone arch bridge. Completed in 1905, it was designed by architect Rudolf Jaussner and built by the engineer Leopold Örley. Each stone block (weighing up to two tons) was individually worked to fit a specific location in Jaussner's design, with the whole thing being assembled on a huge mass of wooden scaffolding. The construction of the arch – meaning, the precise placement of over 5000 tons of stone blocks, with a 12mm layer of cement between them – took just 18 days, and the accuracy of its design was so precise that when the scaffolding was removed, the movement of the arch as it sank slightly under its own massive weight was measured at a mere 6mm.

When the bridge was formally opened in July 1906, Archduke Franz Ferdinand travelled in the first train across – as did Örley, it is said, with a gun held to his head as collateral in case the bridge collapsed. The bridge was blown up by the retreating Austrians during WW1, after which the Italians installed a temporary steel truss. The stone arch was rebuilt in the late 1920s – the only difference being that the original had five arches in each spandrel, as opposed to the present four, and the main arch was a smidgen wider.

Accommodation in Solkan includes the Sabotin Hotel (www.hotel-sabotin.com) and Gostišče Madonca (www.booking.com/hotel/si/madonca-rooms-amp-restaurant), both near the railway station. Primula (www.primula.si) is a good restaurant with a nice terrace, slightly above the town. There are also some extremely good places to eat in Nova Gorica, including Gostilna Metulj (www.gostilna-metulj.si) and the Michelin-starred Dam (www.damhotel.si).

APPENDIX A
Gateway city – Ljubljana

You'll likely pass through Slovenia's beautiful capital, Ljubljana, on your way to or from the Juliana Trail. It's a genuinely wonderful city, and it's well worth stopping there for a night if you have time.

Tourist information
You'll find the main Tourist Information Office at Adamič-Lundrovo nabrežje 2, just across the river from Prešernov trg (www.visitljubljana.com).

Arrival from Ljubljana Airport
Shuttle buses run from outside the terminal building to the train/bus station in the centre of Ljubljana (www.lju-airport.si/en/transport/bus).

Trains and buses
Ljubljana's main railway station (Železniška postaja) is on Masarykova cesta, a 10min walk N from Prešernov trg. The main bus station (Avtobusna postaja) is beside the railway station (timetables at www.ap-ljubljana.si).

Recommended accommodation
Hotel Cubo (www.cubogroup.si), B&B Slamič (www.slamic.si), Hotel Lesar Angel (www.angelhotel.si), One66 Hotel (www.one66hotel.com) and Hotel Park (www.hotel-bb.com).

Recommended restaurants
Slovenska Hiša Figovec (www.figovec.si), Pri Skofu (www.facebook.com/gostilnica.priskofu), Restavracija Cubo (www.cubo.si), Barbarella Juicebar (good little vegetarian and vegan place www.barbarella-juicebar.si) and Gostilna na Gradu (in the castle www.jezersek.si/en/locations/ljubljana-castle).

What to see
Don't miss the 12th-century castle (Ljubljanski grad, www.ljubljanskigrad.si), the River Ljubljanica with its promenades and historic bridges (including the Dragon Bridge and Triple Bridge), the old town with its narrow cobbled streets below the castle, the cathedral, Tivoli Park, and the city's large open market. The work of Jože Plečnik, Slovenia's greatest architect, is dotted across the city and was inscribed on the Unesco World Heritage List in 2021. His former house has been transformed into an excellent museum (Plečnik House, www.mgml.si/en/plecnik-house).

APPENDIX B
Language notes and glossary

The following brief language guide and glossary covers some basic phrases and useful words in Slovene.

Pronunciation

Slovene is a phonetic language, meaning that (unlike English and French for example) every letter in a word is pronounced, and each letter of the alphabet is always pronounced the same way. A few letters have diacritics, and several letters are pronounced differently in Slovene to how they would be in English:

a pronounced as the 'a' in father
c pronounced as the 'ts' in cats
č pronounced as the 'ch' in church
e pronounced as the 'e' in egg
g pronounced hard, as the 'g' in give
i pronounced as the 'i' in ill
j pronounced as the 'y' in yes
o pronounced as the 'o' in hot
r rolled slightly
š pronounced as the 'sh' in shake
u pronounced as the 'oo' in pool
ž pronounced as the 's' in pleasure, or the French 'j' in *janvier*
There is no q, w, x, y

Greetings, introductions and basic phrases

English	Slovenian
Hi / Hello	Živio
Hello / Good day (formal)	Dober dan
Good morning	Dobro jutro
Good evening	Dober večer
Good night	Lahko noč
Goodbye	Na svidenje
Bye (informal)	Adijo
Yes	Ja
No	Ne
Please	Prosim

English	Slovenian
Thank you	Hvala
Thank you very much	Najlepša hvala
You're welcome / Not at all	Prosim / Ni za kaj
Sorry / Excuse me	Oprostite
Do you speak English?	Ali govorite angleško?
I don't speak Slovene	Ne govorim slovensko
How do you say...?	Kako se reče...?
Could you write it down please?	Lahko to napišete?
How are you? (formal / informal)	Kako ste? / Kako si?
Fine, thank you	Dobro, hvala
Where are you from?	Od kod prihajate?
I'm from... (England / Scotland / Ireland / France...)	Sem iz... (anglija / škotska / irska / francija)
Cheers! (as a toast)	Na zdravje!
Where is...?	Kje je...?
Where is the toilet?	Kje je stranišče?
How much does it cost?	Koliko stane?
Can I have the bill, please?	Račun, prosim

General vocabulary

English	Slovenian
beautiful	lep
big	velik
closed	zaprto
difficult	težek
easy	lahek
entrance	vhod
exit	izhod
good	dober

English	Slovenian
open	odprto
possible	mogoče
small	mala
with	z
without	brez

Directions

English	Slovenian
here / there	tu / tam
high / low	visok / nizko
hiking map	planinska karta
on the left / right	na levi / na desni
near / far	blizu / daleč
north / south / east / west	sever / jug / vzhod / zahod
over / under	nad / pod
straight ahead	naravnost

Landscape

English	Slovenian
beach	plaža
cave	jama
cycle path	kolesarska pot
forest	gozd
gorge	soteska
hill	brdo, hrib
karst	kras
lake	jezero
marsh	močvirje
mountain	planina, gora

English	Slovenian
mountain hut	planinska koča
national park	nacionalni park
nature reserve	naravni rezervat
pass	sedlo
path	pot
peak	vrh
ridge	greben
river	reka
rocky	skalnat
sinkhole	vrtača
spring	izvir
stone	kamen
stream	potok
steep	strm
summit	vrh
4x4 track	makadamska cesta
valley	dolina
water	voda
waterfall	slap

Weather

English	Slovenian
cloud	oblak
cloudy	oblačno
cold	mrzel
hail	toča
hot	vroče
ice	led
lightning	strela

English	Slovenian
mist	meglica
rain	dež
sun	sonce
sunny	sončno
snow	sneg
storm / thunderstorm	nevihta
thunder	grmenje
warm	topel
weather	vreme
weather forecast	vremenska napoved
wind	veter

Plants and animals

English	Slovenian
bear	medved
beech	bukev
bird	ptica
butterfly	metulj
chamois	gams
deer	jelen
eagle	orel
flower	cvet
forest	gozd
fox	lisica
snake	kača
spruce	smreka
tree	drevo

Transport

English	Slovenian
airport	letališče
bus	avtobus
bus station	avtobusna postaja
bus stop	postaja
car	avto
platform	peron
railway station	železniška postaja
taxi	taksi
ticket	vozovnica
ticket office	blagajna
train	vlak

Accommodation

English	Slovenian
bathroom	kopalnia
bed	postelja
double room	dvoposteljna soba
guesthouse	gostišče
half board	polpenzion
hostel	hostel
hotel	hotel
mountain hut	planinska koča
room	soba
single room	enoposteljna soba

Food and restaurants (also see menu reader)

English	Slovenian
I'm allergic to…	Alergičen / Alergična sam na…

English	Slovenian
I'm vegetarian	Sem vegetarijanec / vegetarijanka
apple	jabolko
beef	govedina
beer	pivo
bread	kruh
breakfast	zajtrk
cabbage	zelje
cheese	sir
chicken	perutnina
coffee	kava
dinner	večerja
fish	ribe
fruit	sadje
gluten-free	bez glutena
pear	hruška
pub / tavern	gostilna
juice	sok
lunch	kosilo
meat	meso
menu	meni
milk	mleko
mushrooms	gobe
pork	svinjina
potato	krompir
restaurant	restavracija
salad	solata
sausage	klobasa
soup	juha
tea	čaj

English	Slovenian
trout	postrv
vegetables	zelenjava
venison	divjačina
wine	vino

In town

English	Slovenian
bridge	most
castle	grad
cathedral	katedrala
chapel	kapelica
church	cerkev
market	tržnica
museum	muzej
pharmacy	lekarna
post office	pošta
shop	trgovina
square / main square	trg / glavni trg
street	ulica
town / city	grad
tower	stolp
village	selo

Money

English	Slovenian
ATM	bankomat
bank	banka
cash	gotovina
credit card	kreditna kartica

English	Slovenian
exchange office	menjalnica

Timings

English	Slovenian
day	dan
hour	uro
in the morning	zjutraj
in the evening	zvečer
minute	minuta
month	mesec
today	danes
tomorrow	jutri
week	teden
yesterday	včeraj

Dangers and emergencies

English	Slovenian
accident	nesreča
ambulance	reševalno vozilo
blood	krvi
broken bone	reševalno vozilo
Danger!	Pazite!
dentist	zobozdravnik
doctor	zdravnik
emergency medical assistance	nujna medicinska pomoč
fire service	gasilci
first aid	prva pomoč
Help!	Pomoč!
hospital	bolnišnica

English	Slovenian
mountain rescue	gorsko reševanje
police	policia

APPENDIX C
Further reading

Guidebooks

DK Eyewitness *Slovenia* (DK Eyewitness, 2020)

Rudolf Abraham *The Alpe Adria Trail* (Bradt, 2020)

Tadej Koren *The Walk of Peace – A Guide along the Isonzo Front* (Walk of Peace Foundation, 2015)

Janez Bizjak *Triglav National Park* (Mladinska knjiga)

Tine Mihelič & Peter Pehani *Triglav Slovenia's Highest Mountain from all Sides* (Sidarta, 2019)

Justi Carey & Roy Clarke *The Slovene Mountain Trail* (Cicerone, 2023)

Justi Carey & Roy Clarke *The Julian Alps of Slovenia* (Cicerone, 2022)

Natural history

E Nicolas Arnold & Denys W Ovenden *Reptiles and Amphibians of Britain and Europe* (Harper Collins, 2002)

Klaas-Douwe, B Dijkstra & Richard Lewington *Field Guide to the Dragonflies of Britain and Europe* (British Wildlife Publishing, 2006)

Ansgar Hoppe *Flowers of the Alps* (Pelagic Publishing, 2013)

Lars Svensson, Peter J Grant, Killian Mullarney & Dan Zetterström *Collins Bird Guide. 3rd Edition* (Harper Collins, 2023)

Tom Tolman & Richard Lewington *Collins Butterfly Guide* (Harper Collins, 2009)

History

Cathie Carmichael & James Gow *Slovenia and the Slovenes* (C Hurst & Co, 2010)

Florin Curta *Southeastern Europe in the Middle Ages 500–1250* (Cambridge, 2006)

Misha Glenny *The Fall of Yugoslavia* (London, 1992)

Martyn Rady *The Habsburgs: The Rise and Fall of a World Power* (Penguin, 2020)

Martyn Rady *The Habsburg Empire: A Very Short Introduction* (Oxford, 2017)

Laura Silber & Allan Little *The Death of Yugoslavia* (London, 1995)

Peter Štih *The Middle Ages Between the Eastern Alps and the Northern Adriatic: Select Papers on Slovene Historiography and Medieval History* (Brill, 2010)

Mark Thompson *The White War: Life and Death on the Italian Front, 1915-1919* (Faber & Faber, 2009)

Language

Marta Pirnat-Greenberg *Colloquial Slovene* (Routledge, 2015)

APPENDIX D
Contacts and addresses

Embassies
British Embassy
Trg republike 3
1000 Ljubljana
Tel: +386 (0)1 200 39 10
www.gov.uk/world/organisations/
british-embassy-ljubljana

Embassy of Ireland
Palača Kapitelj,
1st floor
Poljanski nasip 6
1000 Ljubljana
Tel: +386 (0)1 300 8970
www.dfa.ie/irish-embassy/slovenia

French Embassy
Barjanska cesta 1
1000 Ljubljana
Tel: +386 (0)1 479 04 00
https://si.ambafrance.org

German Embassy
Prešernova cesta 27
1000 Ljubljana
Tel: +386 (0)1 479 03 00
https://laibach.diplo.de

US Embassy
Prešernova 31
1000 Ljubljana
Tel: +386 (0)1 200 55 00
https://si.usembassy.gov

Local, regional and national tourist offices
Slovenian National Tourist Office
www.slovenia.info/en

Julian Alps
https://julian-alps.com/en

Kranjska Gora Tourist Office
https://kranjska-gora.si/en

Jesenice Tourist Office
www.turizem.jesenice.si/en

Radovljica Tourist Office
www.radolca.si/en

Bled Tourist Office
www.bled.si/en

Bohinj Tourist Office
www.bohinj.si/en

Soča Valley Tourist Office
www.soca-valley.com/en

Goriška Brda Tourist Office
www.brda.si/eng

Visit Ljubljana
www.visitljubljana.com/en

Turismo FVG
www.turismofvg.it/en

Nature
Triglav National Park
www.tnp.si/en/visit

Life Dinalp Bear Project
https://dinalpbear.eu

Life Kočevsko Project
https://life-kocevsko.eu/en

Life Lynx Project
www.lifelynx.eu

Life Wolf Alps Project
www.lifewolfalps.eu/en/project-area/
alpi-slovene

Ministry of the Environment
www.arso.gov.si/en

History
Beekeeping Museum, Radovljica
https://mro.si/en/musem-of-apiculture

Bled Castle
www.blejski-grad.si/en

Iron-making Museum,
Jesenice www.gmj.si/en/
iron-foundry-settlement-stara-sava

Kobarid Museum
www.kobariski-muzej.si/en

Tolmin Museum
www.tol-muzej.si/en

Walk of Peace
www.thewalkofpeace.com

Transport
Slovenian Railways
https://potniski.sz.si/en

Ljubljana Bus Station
www.ap-ljubljana.si/en

Arriva
https://arriva.si/en

Ljubljana Airport
www.lju-airport.si

Local tour operators
Hike & Bike Slovenia
www.hikeandbike.si

Kofler Sport
www.kofler-sport.si/en

Wild Slovenia
www.wild-slovenia.com

Accommodation
The Juliana Trail Booking Centre
https://julian-alps.com

NOTES

DOWNLOAD THE ROUTES
IN GPX FORMAT

All the routes in this guide are available for download from:

www.cicerone.co.uk/1088/GPX

as standard format GPX files. You should be able to load them into most online GPX systems and mobile devices, whether GPS or smartphone. You may need to convert the file into your preferred format using a conversion programme such as gpsvisualizer.com or one of the many other such websites and programmes.

When you follow this link, you will be asked for your email address and where you purchased the guidebook, and have the option to subscribe to the Cicerone e-newsletter.

www.cicerone.co.uk

LISTING OF CICERONE GUIDES

BRITISH ISLES CHALLENGES, COLLECTIONS AND ACTIVITIES

Cycling Land's End to John o' Groats
Great Walks on the England Coast Path
The Big Rounds
The Book of the Bivvy
The Book of the Bothy
The Mountains of England & Wales:
Vol 1 Wales
Vol 2 England
The National Trails
Walking the End to End Trail

SHORT WALKS SERIES

Short Walks Hadrian's Wall
Short Walks in Arnside and Silverdale
Short Walks in Dumfries and Galloway
Short Walks in Nidderdale
Short Walks in the Lake District:
Windermere Ambleside and Grasmere
Short Walks on the Malvern Hills
Short Walks in the Surrey Hills
Short Walks Winchester

SCOTLAND

Ben Nevis and Glen Coe
Cycle Touring in Northern Scotland
Cycling in the Hebrides
Great Mountain Days in Scotland
Mountain Biking in Southern and Central Scotland
Mountain Biking in West and North West Scotland
Not the West Highland Way
Scotland
Scotland's Best Small Mountains
Scotland's Mountain Ridges
Scottish Wild Country Backpacking
Skye's Cuillin Ridge Traverse
The Borders Abbeys Way
The Great Glen Way
The Great Glen Way Map Booklet
The Hebridean Way
The Hebrides
The Isle of Mull
The Isle of Skye
The Skye Trail
The Southern Upland Way
The West Highland Way
The West Highland Way Map Booklet
Walking Ben Lawers, Rannoch and Atholl
Walking in the Cairngorms
Walking in the Pentland Hills
Walking in the Scottish Borders
Walking in the Southern Uplands

Walking in Torridon, Fisherfield, Fannichs and An Teallach
Walking Loch Lomond and the Trossachs
Walking on Arran
Walking on Harris and Lewis
Walking on Jura, Islay and Colonsay
Walking on Rum and the Small Isles
Walking on the Orkney and Shetland Isles
Walking on Uist and Barra
Walking the Cape Wrath Trail
Walking the Corbetts
Vol 1 South of the Great Glen
Vol 2 North of the Great Glen
Walking the Galloway Hills
Walking the John o' Groats Trail
Walking the Munros
Vol 1 – Southern, Central and Western Highlands
Vol 2 – Northern Highlands and the Cairngorms
Winter Climbs: Ben Nevis and Glen Coe

NORTHERN ENGLAND ROUTES

Cycling the Reivers Route
Cycling the Way of the Roses
Hadrian's Cycleway
Hadrian's Wall Path
Hadrian's Wall Path Map Booklet
The Coast to Coast Cycle Route
The Coast to Coast Walk
The Coast to Coast Walk Map Booklet
The Pennine Way
The Pennine Way Map Booklet
Walking the Dales Way
Walking the Dales Way Map Booklet

NORTH-EAST ENGLAND, YORKSHIRE DALES AND PENNINES

Cycling in the Yorkshire Dales
Great Mountain Days in the Pennines
Mountain Biking in the Yorkshire Dales
The Cleveland Way and the Yorkshire Wolds Way
The Cleveland Way Map Booklet
The North York Moors
The Reivers Way
Trail and Fell Running in the Yorkshire Dales
Walking in County Durham
Walking in Northumberland
Walking in the North Pennines
Walking in the Yorkshire Dales: North and East
Walking in the Yorkshire Dales: South and West

Walking St Cuthbert's Way
Walking St Oswald's Way and Northumberland Coast Path

NORTH-WEST ENGLAND AND THE ISLE OF MAN

Cycling the Pennine Bridleway
Isle of Man Coastal Path
The Lancashire Cycleway
The Lune Valley and Howgills
Walking in Cumbria's Eden Valley
Walking in Lancashire
Walking in the Forest of Bowland and Pendle
Walking on the Isle of Man
Walking on the West Pennine Moors
Walking the Ribble Way
Walks in Silverdale and Arnside

LAKE DISTRICT

Bikepacking in the Lake District
Cycling in the Lake District
Great Mountain Days in the Lake District
Joss Naylor's Lakes, Meres and Waters of the Lake District
Lake District Winter Climbs
Lake District: High Level and Fell Walks
Lake District: Low Level and Lake Walks
Mountain Biking in the Lake District
Outdoor Adventures with Children – Lake District
Scrambles in the Lake District – North
Scrambles in the Lake District – South
Trail and Fell Running in the Lake District
Walking The Cumbria Way
Walking the Lake District Fells – Borrowdale
Buttermere
Coniston
Keswick
Langdale
Mardale and the Far East
Patterdale
Wasdale
Walking the Tour of the Lake District

DERBYSHIRE, PEAK DISTRICT AND MIDLANDS

Cycling in the Peak District
Dark Peak Walks
Scrambles in the Dark Peak
Walking in Derbyshire
Walking in the Peak District – White Peak East
Walking in the Peak District – White Peak West

SOUTHERN ENGLAND

20 Classic Sportive Rides in South East England
20 Classic Sportive Rides in South West England
Cycling in the Cotswolds
Mountain Biking on the North Downs
Mountain Biking on the South Downs
Suffolk Coast and Heath Walks
The Cotswold Way
The Cotswold Way Map Booklet
The Kennet and Avon Canal
The Lea Valley Walk
The North Downs Way
The North Downs Way Map Booklet
The Peddars Way and Norfolk Coast Path
The Pilgrims' Way
The Ridgeway National Trail
The Ridgeway National Trail Map Booklet
The South Downs Way
The South Downs Way Map Booklet
The Thames Path
The Thames Path Map Booklet
The Two Moors Way
The Two Moors Way Map Booklet
Walking Hampshire's Test Way
Walking in Cornwall
Walking in Essex
Walking in Kent
Walking in London
Walking in Norfolk
Walking in the Chilterns
Walking in the Cotswolds
Walking in the Isles of Scilly
Walking in the New Forest
Walking in the North Wessex Downs
Walking on Dartmoor
Walking on Guernsey
Walking on Jersey
Walking on the Isle of Wight
Walking the Dartmoor Way
Walking the Jurassic Coast
Walking the South West Coast Path
Walking the South West Coast Path Map Booklets
 – Vol 1: Minehead to St Ives
 – Vol 2: St Ives to Plymouth
 – Vol 3: Plymouth to Poole
Walks in the South Downs National Park

WALES AND WELSH BORDERS

Cycle Touring in Wales
Cycling Lon Las Cymru
Glyndwr's Way
Great Mountain Days in Snowdonia
Hillwalking in Shropshire

Mountain Walking in Snowdonia
Offa's Dyke Path
Offa's Dyke Path Map Booklet
Ridges of Snowdonia
Scrambles in Snowdonia
Snowdonia: 30 Low-level and Easy Walks – North
Snowdonia: 30 Low-level and Easy Walks – South
The Cambrian Way
The Pembrokeshire Coast Path
The Pembrokeshire Coast Path Map Booklet
The Snowdonia Way
The Wye Valley Walk
Walking in Carmarthenshire
Walking in Pembrokeshire
Walking in the Brecon Beacons
Walking in the Forest of Dean
Walking in the Wye Valley
Walking on Gower
Walking the Severn Way
Walking the Shropshire Way
Walking the Wales Coast Path

INTERNATIONAL CHALLENGES, COLLECTIONS AND ACTIVITIES

Europe's High Points
Walking the Via Francigena Pilgrim Route – Part 1

AFRICA

Kilimanjaro
Walking in the Drakensberg
Walks and Scrambles in the Moroccan Anti-Atlas

ALPS CROSS-BORDER ROUTES

100 Hut Walks in the Alps
Alpine Ski Mountaineering Vol 1 – Western Alps
The Karnischer Hohenweg
The Tour of the Bernina
Trail Running – Chamonix and the Mont Blanc region
Trekking Chamonix to Zermatt
Trekking in the Alps
Trekking in the Silvretta and Ratikon Alps
Trekking Munich to Venice
Trekking the Tour of Mont Blanc
Walking in the Alps

PYRENEES AND FRANCE/SPAIN CROSS-BORDER ROUTES

Shorter Treks in the Pyrenees
The GR11 Trail
The Pyrenean Haute Route
The Pyrenees
Walks and Climbs in the Pyrenees

AUSTRIA

Innsbruck Mountain Adventures
Trekking Austria's Adlerweg
Trekking in Austria's Hohe Tauern
Trekking in Austria's Zillertal Alps
Trekking in the Stubai Alps
Walking in Austria
Walking in the Salzkammergut: the Austrian Lake District

EASTERN EUROPE

The Danube Cycleway Vol 2
The Elbe Cycle Route
The High Tatras
The Mountains of Romania
Walking in Hungary

FRANCE, BELGIUM AND LUXEMBOURG

Camino de Santiago – Via Podiensis
Chamonix Mountain Adventures
Cycle Touring in France
Cycling London to Paris
Cycling the Canal de la Garonne
Cycling the Canal du Midi
Cycling the Route des Grandes Alpes
Mont Blanc Walks
Mountain Adventures in the Maurienne
Short Treks on Corsica
The GR5 Trail
The GR5 Trail – Benelux and Lorraine
The GR5 Trail – Vosges and Jura
The Grand Traverse of the Massif Central
The Moselle Cycle Route
The River Loire Cycle Route
The River Rhone Cycle Route
Trekking in the Vanoise
Trekking the Cathar Way
Trekking the GR10
Trekking the GR20 Corsica
Trekking the Robert Louis Stevenson Trail
Via Ferratas of the French Alps
Walking in Provence – East
Walking in Provence – West
Walking in the Ardennes
Walking in the Auvergne
Walking in the Brianconnais
Walking in the Dordogne
Walking in the Haute Savoie: North
Walking in the Haute Savoie: South
Walking on Corsica
Walking the Brittany Coast Path

GERMANY

Hiking and Cycling in the Black Forest
The Danube Cycleway Vol 1

The Rhine Cycle Route
The Westweg
Walking in the Bavarian Alps

IRELAND
The Wild Atlantic Way and
    Western Ireland
Walking the Wicklow Way

ITALY
Alta Via 1 – Trekking in
    the Dolomites
Alta Via 2 – Trekking in
    the Dolomites
Day Walks in the Dolomites
Italy's Grande Traversata delle Alpi
Italy's Sibillini National Park
Ski Touring and Snowshoeing in
    the Dolomites
The Way of St Francis
Trekking in the Apennines
Trekking the Giants' Trail: Alta Via 1
    through the Italian Pennine Alps
Via Ferratas of the Italian Dolomites
    Vols 1&2
Walking and Trekking in the
    Gran Paradiso
Walking in Abruzzo
Walking in Italy's Cinque Terre
Walking in Italy's Stelvio
    National Park
Walking in Sicily
Walking in the Aosta Valley
Walking in the Dolomites
Walking in Tuscany
Walking in Umbria
Walking Lake Como and Maggiore
Walking Lake Garda and Iseo
Walking on the Amalfi Coast
Walking the Via Francigena
    Pilgrim Route – Parts 2&3
Walks and Treks in the
    Maritime Alps

MEDITERRANEAN
The High Mountains of Crete
Trekking in Greece
Walking and Trekking in Zagori
Walking and Trekking on Corfu
Walking in Cyprus
Walking on Malta
Walking on the Greek Islands –
    the Cyclades

NEW ZEALANDANDAUSTRALIA
Hiking the Overland Track

NORTH AMERICA
Hiking and Cycling the California
    Missions Trail
The John Muir Trail
The Pacific Crest Trail

SOUTH AMERICA
Aconcagua and the Southern Andes
Hiking and Biking Peru's Inca Trails
Trekking in Torres del Paine

SCANDINAVIA, ICELAND
AND GREENLAND
Hiking in Norway – South
Trekking in Greenland – The Arctic
    Circle Trail
Trekking the Kungsleden
Walking and Trekking in Iceland

SLOVENIA, CROATIA, SERBIA,
MONTENEGRO AND ALBANIA
Hiking Slovenia's Juliana Trail
Mountain Biking in Slovenia
The Islands of Croatia
The Julian Alps of Slovenia
The Mountains of Montenegro
The Peaks of the Balkans Trail
The Slovene Mountain Trail
Walking in Slovenia: The Karavanke
Walks and Treks in Croatia

SPAIN AND PORTUGAL
Camino de Santiago:
    Camino Frances
Coastal Walks in Andalucia
Costa Blanca Mountain Adventures
Cycling the Camino de Santiago
Cycling the Ruta Via de la Plata
Mountain Walking in Mallorca
Mountain Walking in
    Southern Catalunya
Portugal's Rota Vicentina
Spain's Sendero Historico: The GR1
The Andalucian Coast to Coast Walk
The Camino del Norte and
    Camino Primitivo
The Camino Ingles and Ruta do Mar
The Camino Portugues
The Mountains of Nerja
The Mountains of Ronda
    and Grazalema
The Sierras of Extremadura
Trekking in Mallorca
Trekking in the Canary Islands
Trekking the GR7 in Andalucia
Walking and Trekking in the
    Sierra Nevada
Walking in Andalucia
Walking in Catalunya – Barcelona
Walking in Catalunya – Girona
    Pyrenees
Walking in Portugal
Walking in the Algarve
Walking in the Picos de Europa
Walking on Gran Canaria
Walking on La Gomera and El Hierro
Walking on La Palma
Walking on Lanzarote

and Fuerteventura
Walking on Madeira
Walking on Tenerife
Walking on the Azores
Walking on the Costa Blanca
Walking the Camino dos Faros

SWITZERLAND
Switzerland's Jura Crest Trail
The Swiss Alps
Tour of the Jungfrau Region
Trekking the Swiss Via Alpina
Walking in the Bernese Oberland –
    Jungfrau region
Walking in the Engadine –
    Switzerland
Walking in the Valais
Walking in Ticino
Walking in Zermatt and Saas-Fee

CHINA, JAPAN AND ASIA
Hiking and Trekking in the Japan
    Alps and Mount Fuji
Hiking in Hong Kong
Japan's Kumano Kodo Pilgrimage
Trekking in Tajikistan

HIMALAYA
Annapurna
Everest: A Trekker's Guide
Trekking in Bhutan
Trekking in Ladakh
Trekking in the Himalaya

MOUNTAIN LITERATURE
8000 metres
A Walk in the Clouds
Abode of the Gods
Fifty Years of Adventure
The Pennine Way – the Path,
    the People, the Journey
Unjustifiable Risk?

TECHNIQUES
Fastpacking
Geocaching in the UK
Map and Compass
Outdoor Photography
The Mountain Hut Book

MINI GUIDES
Alpine Flowers
Navigation
Pocket First Aid and
    Wilderness Medicine
Snow

For full information on all our guides,
books and eBooks,
visit our website:
www.cicerone.co.uk